First Published in 2013 by Paleo Media Group LLC
www.paleomediagroup.com

ISBN 13: 978-0-9887172-3-7

The information in this book is not intended to treat, diagnose, cure, or prevent any disease, including digestive problems, and is provided for educational purposes only. The approach proposed in this book is not sponsored, approved, recommended, or endorsed by the FDA, USDA, NIH, or the AND. Always seek the advice of your physician with any questions you have regarding a medical condition, and before undertaking any diet, exercise, or other health program. The author has made her best effort to produce a high-quality, informative, and helpful book, but she makes no representation or warranties of any kind with regard to the completeness or accuracy of the contents of the book.

The author accepts no liability of any kind for any losses or damages caused or alleged to be caused, directly or indirectly, from using the information contained in this book. No part of this publication may be stored in a retrieval system, transmitted, or reproduced in any way, including but not limited to digital copying and printing.

Book design by Kate Miller, Kate Miller Design
Food photography by Savannah Wishart
Foreword by Robb Wolf

Printed in USA

Digestive Health
with REAL Food

the cookbook

100+ anti-inflammatory, nutrient-dense
recipes for optimal health

By Aglaée Jacob, M.S., R.D.

Paleo Media Group
Bend, Oregon

www.PaleoMediaGroup.com

Table of Contents

Recipe Index 6

Foreword 9

Dedication and Acknowledgments 10

Digestive Health with REAL Food 11

Why Is Digestive Health So Important? 12

What Is REAL Food, Exactly? 13

The Protocol 16

How To Use this Book 18

Recipe Master List 23

Breakfasts

    Egg-Free 27

    Egg-Based 35

Snacks, Appetizers and Side Dishes

    Savory 53

    Sweet (but sugar-free) 75

Main Meals

    Chicken 93

    Red Meat 101

    Fish 123

    Variable Protein 133

Flavor Boosters 151

Treats 181

Drinks 205

Ferments 213

Special Projects 221

Index 234

{ breakfasts - egg-free }

28
30
32
46
48

{ breakfasts - egg-based }

36
38
40
42
44
50

{ snacks - savory }

54
56
58
60
62
72
64
66
68
70

{ snacks - sweet }

76
78
80
82
84
86
88
90

120 118 98 96 94

{ mains - chicken }

116 112 108 106 104 102 114 110

{ mains - red meat }

130 128 126 124

{ mains - fish }

148 144 142 146 140 136 138 134

{ mains - protein }

{ flavor boosters }

152
154
156
158
160
162
164
166
168
170
172
174
176
178

{ treats }

182
184
186
188
190
192
194
196
198
200
202

{ drinks }

206
208
210
214
216
218

{ ferments }

{ special projects }

222
224
226
228
230
232

Foreword for *Digestive Health with REAL Food: The Cookbook*

Hey, folks. If you are reading this book, you're probably sick and tired of being sick and tired. Suffering from digestive conditions like irritable bowel syndrome (IBS), inflammatory bowel diseases such as Crohn's and ulcerative colitis, small intestinal bacterial overgrowth (SIBO), celiac disease or leaky gut syndrome is no joke, and these conditions can make life a living hell. Chances are you're also feeling quite a bit overwhelmed. Maybe you thought a quick search on Dr. Google would clear up the confusion, but instead found yourself in an endless loop of conflicting advice.

If you've gone to your doctor for help, you're probably no better off. The traditional recommendation handed out by MDs and nutritionists is to cut the fat and jack up fiber intake. So you ditch red meat and load up on whole grains. Feeling better now? Probably not! The protease inhibitors, lectins, prolamines and gluten (and gluten-like proteins) found in grains are only going to make your plumbing issues worse. Over time, what started off as a "digestive" issue can become a full-blown autoimmune disease as inflammation, food sensitivities and damage to the gut only increase with exposure to grains. The conventional answer to continued symptoms is to start loading you up on prescription medications. Powerful steroids, antispasmodics, antibiotics and other expensive and side-effect-laden substances are now added to the equation, and an already-compromised immune systems and microbiome are sent into further disarray.

Perhaps you've found my book (*The Paleo Solution*) and decided to try a Paleo approach. In the simplest of terms, the Paleo diet is just meat, fish, fowl, vegetables, fruits, roots, tubers and nuts: modern foods that (to the best of our ability) emulate the diets of our pre-agricultural ancestors. Cutting out all grains (and not just the gluten-containing ones!), legumes and dairy likely helped your symptoms, but you're still not all the way there. Maybe you're still enjoying that morning cup of joe, nibbling on dark chocolate, or sipping on a cup of tea. Well, the caffeine found in these otherwise Paleo-friendly foods can irritate digestion and drain your adrenals. How about an afternoon snack of an apple and almonds? Paleo for sure, but also full of FODMAPS, natural sugar alcohols that can contribute to IBS symptoms.

When standard Paleo just isn't enough, that's where *Digestive Health with REAL Food* and the *Digestive Health with Real Food: The Cookbook* by Aglaée Jacob come in. While the first book is the must-read definitive guide to all things intestinal (I referred to it as a "digestive health bible" when I reviewed it on my website), the second is a collection of recipes that take all the guesswork out of cooking gut-friendly meals. Why is having a cookbook like this so important? The bottom line is that for any diet-based health intervention to work, it has to make sense, it has to be livable, and it has to be good. Whether it's the grain-free Bananoatmeal, Roasted Bone Marrow and Grilled Fruit Kebabs, or Gummy Yummies, every recipe is not only delicious, but it's designed with your digestive health in mind. Aglaée also includes how-to guides for pickling, fermenting, and starting your own SCOBY. What the heck is a SCOBY, you ask? Just keep reading, and you'll find out (and want to grow one) soon enough!

Robb Wolf
New York Times Best Selling Author of *The Paleo Solution*

Dedication

To everyone dealing with digestive issues and spending too much time wondering what they can and cannot eat. I hope this book extends your culinary horizons and fuels your creativity in the kitchen by helping you get back to the basics of cooking with REAL food.

Gratitude

First and foremost, I am grateful to *you*. This project wouldn't have been possible without the interest you showed in my first book, *Digestive Health with REAL Food: A Practical Guide to an Anti-Inflammatory, Low-Irritant, Nutrient-Dense Diet for IBS & Other Digestive Issues*. Since its release, thousands of people have finally been able to improve their digestion and overall health simply by using REAL food as medicine.

I'm very grateful to all of you who took the time to share your success stories with me. My goal with my first book was to help people like you start living a better life, free from digestive issues. Having walked this path myself, I know there's nothing more important in life than health—and nothing more important to health than digestive health. Not only did I reach my goal, but I feel like the message is only starting to spread. Thank you for believing in REAL food!

A special acknowledgment to Cain Credicott, editor of *Paleo Magazine*, for enthusiastically helping me make this project happen. I also want to thank the team that was part of the success of my first book, *Digestive Health with REAL Food*, and that I'm sure will help make this companion cookbook another success. Special thanks to Ray Sylvester, editor, Kate Miller, graphic designer, and Savannah Wishart, food photographer. I'm so grateful I could have you all on my team again for this cookbook!

Merci à ma famille et amis pour croire en moi! Un merci tout spécial à mes parents Hélène et Gilles et à mon frère Ludovic ainsi qu'à ma belle-famille Jean, Johanne, Mélissa et Anouk. Bien qu'on soit souvent loin en distance, vous êtes toujours prêts de mon coeur.

Finally, I couldn't have done it without my always loving and supportive husband, Jonathan. Your help and support were precious, especially on the difficult days where I felt like I couldn't do it all. Thanks for always bringing the best out of me. Je t'aime tellement mon amour!

Digestive Health with REAL Food

When I started suffering from my own digestive issues, I knew they had to be connected to what I was eating. It just seemed to make sense that the food you put in your digestive tract could directly affect the way you feel, especially when it comes to symptoms like bloating, abdominal pain and bowel movement changes.

Even as a registered dietitian with hundreds of hours of training and practice in nutrition, I felt like I didn't have the tools I needed to help myself or my clients when it came to digestive health. The low-fat, high-fiber, whole-grain, "everything in moderation" approach I had been taught wasn't doing it. This spurred me on my quest to learn more about gastroenterology—and I started by reading every book and scientific study I could get my hands on.

There's Hope!

After many months of hard work, with myself and with clients around the world suffering from similar digestive issues, I began to gather evidence and experience. I learned how many people out there were struggling with their digestion and unable to get relief despite the advice of doctors or dietitians who told them to eat less fat and more fiber. I wanted to find a way to reach out to those people, who had been left with no other choice but to suffer in silence, to let them know that there is hope.

Because there is hope. For you, too. Even if you feel like you've tried everything under the sun, you might not have had all the information you needed to make your past attempts successful. Maybe you tried a gluten-free diet, a dairy-free diet, a low-FODMAP diet or even a Paleo diet. Even though any of these dietary modifications can often help people improve their digestive health, neither of them might have been the right approach for you.

What's Different About the *Digestive Health with REAL Food* Approach?

How do you know if the *Digestive Health with REAL Food* (*DHwRF*) approach is right for you? The fact that it worked beautifully for me and hundreds of other people might be encouraging, but it doesn't offer any guarantee that it will do the same for you. While many other books about digestive health recommend very specific dietary changes to heal your ailments—whether through a gluten-free diet, a wheat-free diet, a low-FODMAP diet, a dairy-free diet or a Paleo diet—I don't pretend to know exactly what kind of diet is right for you.

Rather, the *DHwRF* approach guides you on a journey to discover that diet for yourself. Everybody is different, and I can't claim to know exactly what type of diet is best for you, but I can give you the tools to figure it out by yourself.

The foods that will be part of your optimal diet might not be the same as someone else's, even if you're dealing with exactly the same symptoms. Following a holistically designed elimination diet is the best way to first get your digestive symptoms under control and, secondly, to build your own optimal diet—the diet that will help you get rid of the irritation and inflammation in your intestines, while nourishing your whole body to allow your gut to heal and your quality of life to reach a whole new level.

Why Is Digestive Health So Important?

Your digestive health is worth fighting for. Any of these digestive issues:

- IBS (irritable bowel syndrome)
- Fructose malabsorption
- FODMAP intolerance
- Small intestinal bacterial overgrowth (SIBO)
- Celiac disease
- Crohn's disease
- Ulcerative colitis
- Food intolerances with an unknown cause
- Any other digestive problem

…is a sign that your body is reacting to something—and it's trying to let you know. Besides the impact they can have on your quality of life and well-being, digestive problems like bloating, abdominal pain, constipation, diarrhea and other digestive symptoms can interfere with your overall health beyond the bathroom.

Even if you "just" have IBS and your doctor told you that your intestines were "perfectly fine," chronic digestive issues can cause even more health problems in the long term. If you have problems with digestion, you can assume that you have some sort of damage in your gastrointestinal (GI) tract, whether or not it's visible to your doctor. This damage can result in:

- **Chronic low-grade inflammation** that can affect your whole body, potentially causing **weight problems** (underweight or overweight) in some people
- **Malnutrition** resulting from an inadequate absorption of the nutrients (protein, healthy fats, vitamins and minerals) in the food you eat
- **Impaired intestinal permeability**, also known as **leaky gut**, that can put you at higher risk of developing an autoimmune condition (or worsening an existing one)
- **Mood imbalances** such as depression and anxiety
- **Poor immunity**, leaving you more vulnerable to illness from microbes you encounter
- **Systemic symptoms** that can affect almost every part of your body, including:
  - fatigue, brain fog and difficulty concentrating
  - aches and pains
  - skin problems (such as acne or eczema)
  - asthma and other respiratory problems
  - headaches and migraines
  - infertility

Hippocrates said over 2,000 years ago that *"health starts in the gut"*—and he couldn't have been more right. And the best way to optimize your digestive health is with REAL food.

What Is REAL Food, Exactly?

REAL food is food that can be found easily in nature and consumed after minimal processing. REAL food is easy to digest, anti-inflammatory, nutrient dense, and low in irritants and allergens. REAL food is what your body would crave if you allowed it to wean off processed foods that overstimulate your taste buds, your brain and your hormones. REAL food is food that is less likely to trigger digestive symptoms. And finally, REAL food is food that will allow your gut to heal and your whole body to reach its optimal health state.

The REAL foods that are right for you may vary, but should include:

- **Animal protein**, especially from pastured animals fed a species-appropriate diet (such as grass-fed beef, grass-fed bison, pastured chicken, pastured pork, wild-caught fish and seafood, and pastured eggs)

- **Traditional fats**, because of their stable fatty acids and high nutrient density (such as coconut oil, ghee, butter, tallow, lard, olive oil and avocado)

- **Plant matter**, because of the antioxidants, vitamins and minerals they add to your diet (such as vegetables, fruits, tubers, nuts and coconut)

- **Tasty seasonings**, because they can spice up your diet without the need for processed and artificial ingredients (such as herbs, spices, vinegar and unrefined salt)

Free of All the Bad Stuff!

All the recipes in this cookbook are made with REAL food ingredients. All the recipes are free of grains, dairy, legumes, soy, and refined ingredients. Most of them are low in FODMAPs and free of nightshades, and you'll also find many nut-free and egg-free recipes. This cookbook offers a variety of ideas to suit all kinds of dietary restrictions.

Problematic Foods

Despite what you might have been told by the medical community, what you eat can greatly affect your digestive health, for better or worse. No matter your specific digestive problems, you've probably noticed that some foods can trigger bloating, abdominal pain, diarrhea or constipation. It can sometimes be difficult to identify the foods that are problematic for you, but here's a list of the most common ones. (see next page)

Foods	Potentially Problematic Ingredients*		Notes
Grains	Gluten	Wheat, barley, rye, most oats	Grains, whether or not they contain gluten, are usually found in a highly processed form and are poor in health-supporting nutrients.
	Carbs (starches)	Bread, pasta, breakfast cereals, rice, oatmeal, crackers, cookies	
	Processed ingredients		
	FODMAPs*	Wheat, barley and rye	
Legumes	Protein	Soy, peanuts	Legumes do not contain any nutrients that you cannot obtain from other foods.
	FODMAPs*	Beans and lentils	
	Carbs (starches)	Beans and lentils	
Refined Oils	High-omega-6 fats	Corn oil, soybean oil, peanut oil, sunflower oil, safflower oil, canola oil, vegetable oil, margarines, shortenings, processed foods	Omega-6 fats can be inflammatory. Instead, use low-omega-6 fats like ghee, coconut oil, tallow, lard, avocado and olive oil.
Processed Foods	Carbs (sugars)	Anything that comes in a box or contains unpronounceable ingredients: bread, sauces, cookies, crackers, sugary lattes, burgers, frozen meals, bars	Processed carbohydrates can cause imbalances in your gut flora, while refined ingredients can irritate your digestive system. Processed foods are also devoid of healing nutrients.
	Processed ingredients (artificial sweeteners, monosodium glutamate, etc.)		
Dairy	Lactose (FODMAP*)	Milk, fresh cheese, commercial yogurt, ice cream	Casein can irritate the digestive system of some people.
	Casein (protein)	Milk, cheese, yogurt	

* This list is non-exhaustive; please refer to the book *DHwRF* for more details.
** FODMAPs stand for **f**ermentable **o**ligo-, **d**i-, **m**ono-saccharides **a**nd **p**olyols.;

Category	Potentially Problematic Ingredients		Notes
Alcohol	Gluten	Any alcohol made from wheat, rye or barley (beer, non-distilled alcohol)	Many people are sensitive to gluten.
	Alcohol	All alcoholic beverages	Alcohol can cause leaky gut.
	Carbs (sugars)	Beer, wine, cocktails	Carbs can feed an imbalance in your gut flora.
Caffeine	Caffeine	All coffees, energy drinks, colas, dark chocolate, black tea	Caffeine can irritate your digestive system and fatigue your adrenals.
	Processed ingredients (sugar, artificial sweeteners, flavorings)	Sweetened coffees, mochas, flavored coffees, hot chocolates and other blended beverages	Processed ingredients can irritate your digestive system and sugars can alter your gut flora.
	Dairy (casein, lactose)	Lattes, cappuccinos	Dairy is a common source of food intolerances.
Vegetables	Nightshades	White potato, tomato, eggplant, bell pepper, hot pepper, chili powder, paprika, curry	Nightshades contain glycoalkaloids that can irritate your digestive system and contribute to a leaky gut.
	FODMAPs*	Onion, garlic, broccoli, cabbage, cauliflower, okra, mushrooms, avocado, artichoke	If your gut flora is unbalanced, FODMAP-containing vegetables might cause digestive problems.
Tubers	Carbs (starches)	Sweet potatoes, white potatoes rutabaga, yucca (cassava)	Starches can be difficult to digest if your gut lining is irritated. They can also feed a gut flora imbalance.
	FODMAPs*	Sweet potatoes	Can cause digestive problems if your gut flora is compromised.

Category	Potentially Problematic Ingredients		Notes
Fruits	**FODMAPs**	Apples, pears, watermelon, stone fruits (nectarines, peaches, plums), blackberries, dried fruits	If your gut flora is unbalanced, FODMAP-containing fruits and all other natural sugars found in fruits might cause digestive problems.
	Carbs (sugars)	All fruits	
Eggs	**Protein**	Egg whites and egg yolks	Can cause reaction in some people, especially those with a leaky gut.
Nuts	**Protein**	Almonds, cashews macadamia, hazelnuts, pistachios	Can cause reactions in some people, especially those with a leaky gut.
	FODMAPs	Almonds, pistachios, cashews and hazelnuts	Can cause digestive problems if your gut flora is compromised.
Seeds	**Protein**	Sunflower seeds (sunbutter), sesame seeds (tahini), flaxseeds, coffee, cocoa (chocolate)	Can cause reaction in some people, especially those with a leaky gut.
Spices	**Seeds** (protein)	Nutmeg, cumin seeds, anise seeds, black caraway seeds, mustard seeds	Can cause reaction in some people, especially those with a leaky gut.
	Nightshades	Chili powder, ketchup, cayenne, hot pepper, curry, tomato paste	Nightshades contain glycoalkaloids that can irritate your digestive system and contribute to a leaky gut.

* This list is non-exhaustive; please refer to the book *DHwRF* for more details.
** FODMAPs stand for **f**ermentable **o**ligo-, **d**i-, **m**ono-saccharides **a**nd **p**olyols.;

Note that grains and legumes should be considered processed foods, despite the fact that they grow in nature. This is because they require extensive processing before they reach your plate. In the case of wheat or soy, for example, you can't eat them directly from the field, as you can with most vegetables and fruits. A simple look at the labels of foods containing these ingredients will convince you that they're not REAL foods. The same can be said of dairy, especially when it comes from cows that are confined indoors and fed grains (cows should eat only grass!), and if dairy products are pasteurized (high temperatures change their composition) and supplemented with processed ingredients.

Gut-Healing, Nutrient-Dense, Anti-Inflammatory REAL Food

Removing the most common problematic foods by following the elimination diet protocol will help you better manage your digestive symptoms. But we'll also go a step further. Beyond controlling your digestive symptoms, it's also important to incorporate foods and lifestyle strategies that will help you decrease the inflammation, correct nutrient deficiencies and heal your gut so you can achieve optimal digestive health. Read the ingredients section (pp. 18-22) to learn more about these foods.

The *Digestive Health with REAL Food* Protocol

This cookbook is designed to be a companion to the book of the same name. You can of course use this cookbook by itself and find great relief from your digestive problems by eliminating many potentially problematic foods and basing your diet on REAL food. But if you want to better understand the whys, the whats and the hows, the original *DHwRF* book will give you all the information you need to better understand the *DHwRF* approach.

In addition to understanding what might be going wrong with your digestion and learning about the relationship between food and your digestive symptoms, you'll also get all the information you need to troubleshoot problems that may arise on your path to better digestive health, so you can finally make some sense of how a proper elimination diet should be implemented.

In a nutshell, the elimination diet protocol explained in *DHwRF* includes two main phases:
1) the elimination phase and
2) the reintroduction phase.

The Elimination Phase: Eliminate Your Symptoms

The elimination phase is the strictest phase of the protocol, but it's the most effective way to get your symptoms under control as quickly as possible. The elimination phase is not aimed at eliminating foods from your diet, but eliminating symptoms from your life. Doesn't it sound more appealing that way?

Removing potentially problematic foods (pp. 13-15) such as grains, legumes, sugars and processed foods can be a daunting and difficult—but necessary—first step toward reducing inflammation, irritation and excessive fermentation in your digestive tract. You may not necessarily be sensitive to all the foods you remove, and you may not need to keep them out of your diet forever, but removing them allows you to start from the best baseline before moving on to the reintroduction phase.

Think of it this way: Let's say you're cooking your favorite spaghetti sauce and are trying to adjust the seasonings. If you add all the seasonings in your cupboard all at once, it will be hard to determine whether you like the combination of oregano, thyme and basil better, whether a little more salt would be best, or if you prefer your sauce without any parsley. How could you tell with such chaos? The best way to save your recipe would be to make a fresh batch of your spaghetti sauce with no seasonings to taste it plain. Once you have a good baseline to start with, you can add seasonings one at a time, starting with small amounts and increasing them gradually, tasting each time, until you find the perfect balance.

It's exactly the same with an elimination protocol. You have to do a bit of cleaning in your diet to return to a safe baseline that will almost certainly make you feel a lot better more quickly. From this starting point, you'll be able to build your personal optimal diet during the reintroduction phase.

Recipes that are appropriate for the elimination phase are clearly labeled at the top of each recipe page. You can also find them in the recipe master list. You may also be able to modify other recipes in this book to remove or replace ingredients that aren't appropriate for you right now. For most people, the elimination phase lasts about three to four weeks and results in great improvements in their digestive symptoms. After that point, it's time to move to the reintroduction phase.

The Reintroduction Phase: Building Your Optimal (BYO) Diet

During the reintroduction phase, you'll be able to have a little bit of fun with new recipes. Once you have completed the elimination phase and your digestive symptoms are under control, you can reintroduce a new food every three or four days to assess your tolerance to it. Because REAL food is so nutrient-dense, anti-inflammatory and good for you, I recommend that you focus on these foods during the reintroduction phase because your gut still has some healing to do. Choosing REAL food will help your body continue this healing process while adding variety and fun to your diet.

Examples of REAL food you can test during this phase include eggs, nuts, some FODMAP-containing foods like onions and broccoli, starches like sweet potatoes, and natural sugars found in fruits. *DHwRF* gives you more details about the pros and cons of these different food categories, but the only information that really matters for the reintroduction phase is the information that your own body will be giving you. After going through the elimination phase and returning to a safe baseline of stability in your digestive symptoms, your body will be able to more clearly let you know what it likes and what it doesn't. Just like making your spaghetti sauce by adding seasonings one at a time to make sure it tastes perfect.

You can find inspiration to determine what REAL foods you want to reintroduce by looking at the Recipe Master List (pp. 23-25). Then find a recipe that contains those specific ingredients (and excludes any other ingredients you don't tolerate, of course). Or use the browsing method, and peruse the beautiful recipe photos in the cookbook. You'll always find a clear label at the top of the page indicating what special ingredients (that aren't part of the elimination phase) are used for each recipe. The good news is that most of the recipes in this cookbook are simple and have a short ingredient list, so they should fit most anyone's diet regardless of their specific dietary restrictions.

How To Use this Book

I hope you use this book to keep you inspired in your journey to better digestive health. I know it can often feel daunting to prepare your meals when you only have a restricted list of foods. Even if you're on the strictest phase of the elimination diet, you don't have to eat the same things all the time. The beauty of REAL food is that it's so versatile. Cutting and cooking things a different way, and combining them with different traditional fats and tasty seasonings can give you a variety of delicious gut-friendly options to choose from. This cookbook already provides more than 100 recipes, but you can create hundreds of different meals by making simple substitutions in the fats, seasonings and side dishes you incorporate. Use the recipe master list (pp. 23-25) to find recipes that fit your dietary restrictions.

Over one-third of the recipes are appropriate for the elimination phase. Almost all of the recipes are free of dairy and sugars. Some recipes contain FODMAPs, but you can usually easily substitute the FODMAP-containing ingredients for some that you tolerate better. And a few recipes have eggs, starches, nuts and nightshades. All the recipes are labeled to let you know whether they're safe to use during the elimination phase. If not, you'll find a clear description of the recipe's ingredients to see at a glance if the recipe fits your diet.

Even though you won't be able to enjoy all the recipes when you're following the strict elimination phase, you'll still have more than 25 recipes to get you started (in addition to the more than 20 in the original *DHwRF* book). You can use the other recipes that you can't yet make to find inspiration for your reintroduction challenges, to give you something to look forward to once your gut has healed, and to feed the rest of your family if you're trying to transition them to a REAL food diet.

Think Outside the Box!

You'll find that recipes are classified as breakfasts, snacks, main meals or desserts—but take these categories with a grain of salt. Ideally, I would have labeled them all as "just food!" Any main meals can be eaten for breakfasts, desserts and breakfast can be snacks and you can use the breakfast ideas as a main meal. Just don't use the treats as the foundation of your diet of course! Customize the recipes to suit the personal optimal diet you build by following the *DHwRF* approach.

You Can't Go Wrong with REAL Ingredients

Also remember that the recipes are very versatile, and you can usually substitute the protein, vegetables and seasonings to your liking to create your own specialties. Have fun in the kitchen, and don't be afraid to use your imagination! Use the recipes as guidelines and follow your inspiration. Even if you don't have a lot of experience in the kitchen, you can't really go wrong if you use REAL food. The hardest part is probably the seasonings. Add them little by little, and taste often to make sure they're just right. You can even take notes on your favorite seasoning combinations at the same time, directly in the book or on a notepad, so you have a guide next time you do the recipe.

Your culinary skills play only a small role in how your meals turn out. The biggest factor is the quality of your ingredients. The more you know about where your food comes from, the more delicious and nutritious your meals will be. And the good news is that by choosing REAL food, you won't have to read any complicated labels or nutrition tables. And don't worry about calories or fat grams—simply focus on the quality of the ingredients.

Let's look at what you need to know to find the most nutrient- and taste-dense REAL foods. The four staple ingredient categories that follow will allow you to prepare healthy meals that support gut healing:

animal protein + traditional fats + plant matter + tasty seasonings

Ingredient #1: Animal Protein

Protein from animal sources is superior to that from vegetarian sources (such as beans, lentils and soy) in many ways. In addition to not containing problematic ingredients that could irritate your gut or feed a gut dysbiosis, animal protein foods are rich in nutrients that can help you regain your health. Quality is paramount, though. You've probably heard the saying, "You are what you eat," but it should actually be modified to "you are what you eat eats" (credit: Michael Pollan). If you want to take eating REAL food one step further, it's time to ask questions and play detective to find out where your food really comes from.

Most of the meat, eggs, fish and dairy products found at the grocery store come from not-so-healthy animals fed a species-inappropriate diet. Do you think it's natural for cows to eat wheat and corn? For chicken to be deprived of bugs and worms? For fish to eat soy? And what about the fact that these animals are often raised in crowded conditions with little or no contact with nature or sunlight? Not only do these "modern" feeding practices pose problems for the animals' health, they also affect your own health and the health of the planet.

Happy, healthy animals fed a species-appropriate diet contain more anti-inflammatory omega-3 fats, anti-cancer CLA fatty acids, and other important nutrients and antioxidants like vitamins A, D, E and the Bs, as well as iron, zinc and selenium. And all of that nutritional goodness is naturally free of hormones or antibiotics.

To find high-quality animal protein, get out of the grocery store and visit your local butcher or farmers market. In the USA, visit eatwild.com, localharvest.org or U.S. Wellness Meats (grasslandbeef.com). Anywhere in the world, you can contact your local chapter of the Weston A. Price Foundation (westonaprice.org) or visit your local farmers market.

If you can't find or afford grass-fed beef or eggs from pastured chickens, don't stress too much about it. For one, stress is no good for your digestive health! And the meat and eggs commonly found at the grocery store are not necessarily bad for you—it's just that the grass-fed and pastured options offer an extra nutritional boost. If you eat animal protein from the grocery store, try to choose the highest quality sources of the other REAL foods in your diet. It might also be a good idea to go for leaner cuts of meat and to trim excess fat. This is not because fat is bad for your health, but because the fats found in grain-fed meat raised in confined animal feeding operations (CAFOs) have a higher omega-6 to omega-3 ratio than grass-fed and pastured animal protein, and can thus have a more inflammatory effect on your body. If your budget is limited or you simply don't have access to high-quality meats, all you need to do is get less fat from your meat and more from other sources (see the fat section below).

Be aware that pastured and grass-fed meat tends to be leaner and cook more quickly, but you should be able to adjust fairly easily. Also keep in mind that the taste is a bit different. Some people describe it as being more "gamey," but I personally think of it as "tasty"! In my opinion, beef and chicken from the grocery store are pretty bland. Grass-fed beef and pastured chicken are a lot more flavorful because they're full of the nutrients they're meant to contain.

You'll see that some recipes ask for gelatin (or suggest it as an addition), such as the Coconut Yogurt (recipe, p. 214), Tummy Gummies (recipe, p. 86), Energy Tea Latte (recipe, p. 208) and Speedy Recovery Soup (recipe, p. 134). While any powdered gelatin will work equally well, I prefer choosing the highest-quality gelatin from healthy pastured animals. The only company that meets these criteria at the time of writing this cookbook is Great Lakes Gelatin Company (greatlakesgelatin.com). If you can't get it, any other powdered gelatin at your grocery store will still provide more good than bad.

You'll also find that a few of the recipes use organ meats, such as heart, tongue, bone marrow and liver. Often referred to as "nasty bits," organ meats are some of the most nutrient-dense parts of any animal. Don't look down on them! Did you know that hunter-gatherers used to eat the organs first and leave the leftover muscle meat as scrap food for their dogs? Our ancestors intuitively knew where to get their nutrition. And you shouldn't eat nasty bits only for their nutritional value; they're also a delicacy. Renowned chefs around the world appreciate these once-prized parts for their unique taste and texture. Cooking organ meat can be scary at first. I know—I was once in your shoes. I didn't grow up eating any of these things, but I've learned to love them! When you feel ready, try going beyond your comfort zone and experiment with these recipes: Anticuchos (recipe, p. 108), Bison Multivitamin (recipe, p. 120), Liver Pâté (recipe, p.120), Roasted Bone Marrow (recipe, p. 68), Mellow Marrow (recipe, p. 30), Fajitas de Lengua (recipe, p. 114) and Homemade Bone Broth (recipe, p. 176). You won't regret it!

Ingredient #2: Traditional Fats

For a while, people have been misled to believe that fats are empty calories. It's true that vegetable oils like canola oil, soybean oil, peanut oil, cottonseed oil, corn oil, sunflower oil and safflower oil are almost completely devoid of vitamins and minerals after the extensive refining process they go through. But this is not the case for traditional fats, an underexploited gold mine of nourishment.

Animal fats like lard, tallow, duck fat, butter, ghee, and fats from meats and egg yolks provide good sources of vitamins E, A and D, coenzyme Q10 (CoQ10), choline and many other fat-soluble antioxidants. This is especially true if the fats come from happy and healthy pastured animals. See the animal protein section above to find the best sources, and try the Ghee (recipe, p. 160) and Grass-Fed Tallow (recipe, p. 174) recipes to make your own healthy traditional fats.

Some vegetable sources of fats also belong to the traditional fats category because of their minimal processing, high stability and superior nutrient density. Such fats include coconut oil, red palm oil, olive oil, macadamia oil and avocado oil. While coconut and red palm oil are stable enough to be used for cooking, the other oils should be kept for cold use only. For all of these oils, the less processed, the better. For example, cold-pressed and extra-virgin will ensure that you get the best-quality fats—they're less likely to be oxidized or rancid, as is often the case with most conventionally extracted vegetable and seed oils—and more of the natural nutrients they have to offer.

Other coconut-derived products like unsweetened coconut flesh, coconut milk and coconut butter can also contribute to your daily fat intake and help you obtain a greater variety of nutrients your body needs to support the healing process. Choose organic whenever you can. In the case of coconut milk, make sure you choose a brand that doesn't include any thickeners, as guar gum, xanthan gum and carrageenan can be problematic for people suffering from digestive problems.

Note that although all of these fats are more stable than refined, high-omega-6 vegetable oils, some are more suited for tolerating higher temperatures. Although most recipes call for ghee or coconut oil, you can use any of the traditional fats below interchangeably within their respective category.

> - **Stable cooking fats:** Coconut oil, ghee, butter, tallow, lard, duck fat and palm oil
> - **For cold uses only**: Olive oil, avocado oil and macadamia oil (to preserve their fragile antioxidants)

Ingredient #3: Plant Matter—Vegetables, Fruits, Tubers and Nuts

Where your food comes from matters just as much with plants as it does with animal protein and traditional fats. Here are a few tips to ensure you are protecting yourself against potentially harmful pesticides and chemical products that are commonly used in "modern" agriculture.

Is organic worth it? Usually. But know that looking for the organic label isn't the only way to ensure safe food. Visit your local farmers market or join a CSA (community-supported agriculture) and ask about their agricultural practices. Even if a farm doesn't have the budget to go through the formalities required to obtain an organic label, their produce may still easily meet, or exceed, the "organic" criteria. And don't be afraid to ask—it's your right to know.

If access to chemical-free local produce is limited and you don't want to break the bank by buying everything organic, consult the table below to decide which produce is worth the extra bucks ("dirtiest" options in the right column) and which are safest to buy non-organic ("cleanest" options in the left column).

Vegetables are also very easy to grow—season permitting, of course. All you need is a small piece of land or a few big pots on your balcony. Joining a community garden is also a possibility if this option is available in your area. Planting a small garden can allow you to save a bit of money and gain even more nutritional value from your vegetables by maximizing their freshness (and therefore nutrient density) and protecting yourself from chemicals.

Cleanest Least contaminated • Safe to buy non-organic	Dirtiest Most contaminated • Avoid or buy organic only
• Asparagus • Avocado • Cabbage • Cantaloupe • Sweet corn • Eggplant • Grapefruit • Kiwi • Mango • Mushrooms • Onions • Papaya • Pineapple • Sweet peas (frozen) • Sweet potato • Watermelon	• Apples • Celery • Cherry tomatoes • Cucumber • Grapes • Hot peppers • Nectarines (imported) • Peaches • Potatoes • Spinach • Strawberries • Sweet bell peppers • Kale/collard greens • Summer squash (zucchini) • Blueberries (domestic) • Lettuce

*Adapted from the Environmental Working Group's *2013 Shopper's Guide to Pesticides in Produce*,
available at www.ewg.org/foodnews/summary.php.

Ingredient #4: Tasty Seasonings

Spices and herbs (fresh or dried) are unfortunately often contaminated with residues of pesticides, other chemicals, fungi or mycotoxins. Because dried herbs and spices are very concentrated parts of the plant, the chemical content can therefore add up quite quickly. For that reason, it might be worth going organic for your seasonings.

If you decide to invest in good-quality seasonings, it's important to know how to care for them. Your spices and dried herbs will keep best in a hermetic container away from heat and light. To maximize the flavor and antioxidant content of your seasonings, only buy small quantities at a time and replace them every six months to a year.

While seasonings are optional in the recipes in this cookbook, they're a great way to add more variety and fun to your meals. The only exception to the rule is salt. Despite the bad press it's gotten, sodium, the main mineral found in salt, occupies an important place on your plate when eating a REAL food diet for better digestive health. But not just any kind of salt will do. White table salt is extensively refined, stripped of all of its minerals (besides sodium), and supplemented with questionable anticaking agents to make the salt "flow" better, before finally being bleached with chemicals. Nothing like REAL food...

Instead, look for unrefined or natural salts. These salts provide a variety of minerals, are free of chemicals and have a much more pleasant taste. Sea salt and Celtic sea salt are two great unrefined-salt options. If you want to further minimize the risk of exposure to some of the contaminants now found in the sea, go for Himalayan salt, Hawaiian salt, Murray River salt from Australia or other unrefined salts harvested directly from nature.

The Seasoning Safe List*	Seasonings to Experiment With**
• Unrefined salt • Chives • Asafoetida powder • Cinnamon • Lemon or lime juice • Apple cider vinegar • Ginger • Fresh herbs (basil, rosemary, thyme, parsley, peppermint, sage, tarragon, oregano, dill, cilantro, bay leaves) • Green part of green onions (small amounts, FODMAP-free) • Garlic-infused ghee or oil (FODMAP-free, see recipe, p. 162) • Herb-infused oil (see recipe, p. 178)	• Balsamic vinegar (ideally aged and sugar free) • Red wine vinegar • Pepper (black, pink, white and other peppercorns) • Hot peppers, chili powder, Tabasco sauce • Curry powder, paprika (nightshades) • Coconut aminos • Tamari sauce (wheat- and gluten-free) • Sun-dried tomatoes (nightshade) • Onions and garlic (FODMAPs; in salad dressings and mayonnaise) • Sea vegetables (kelp, nori) • Nutmeg, anise seeds, black caraway seeds, celery seeds, cumin seeds, dill seeds, fennel seeds, fenugreek, mustard and poppy seeds (seeds)

*These choices are usually safe for most people, but it's not impossible to react to them; avoid any items you know you are sensitive to;
**You can experiment with these seasonings during the reintroduction phase of your elimination diet.

Quality Matters!

Try using the best-quality ingredients you can afford. Consider it an investment in your own health. Use the chart below to find the best options.

REAL Foods		Best	In-Between	Okay
Animal Protein	Beef and bison	Pastured, 100% grass-fed and grass-finished	Organic	Conventional, but lean cuts only (or trim the fat)
	Pork	Pastured		
	Poultry and eggs	Pastured and free-run		Conventional but without the skin
	Fish and seafood	Wild-caught		Conventional
Traditional Fats	Coconut oil	Virgin or cold-pressed organic	Virgin or cold-pressed	Regular
	Palm oil	Organic, red and unrefined	Red and unrefined	
	Animal fat (lard, tallow, duck fat, ghee, butter, etc.)	From pastured, 100% grass-fed animal	Organic	Regular
	Olive, macadamia and avocado oils*	Extra-virgin, cold-pressed and organic	Organic	Regular
	Coconut milk	Organic and free of thickeners	Free of thickeners	Regular
Plant Matter	Vegetables	Organic (chemical-free) and local	Least-contaminated produce (see p. 20)	Conventional (some plant matter is better than none!)
	Fruits			
	Tubers			
	Nuts and seeds			
Seasonings	Salt	Unrefined: Himalayan salt, Celtic sea salt, etc.	Sea salt	Table salt
	Herbs and spices	Organic, or grown in your own garden	-	Regular

*These oils should ideally not be used for cooking, but only for cold uses.

Ready? Let's get cooking!

		Recipes	page	Elimination Phase	Eggs	Coconut	Nuts	Nightshades	FODMAPs	New veggies	Fruits	Starch	Sugar	Other
Breakfasts	Egg-Free	Bananoatmeal	28			✓					✓			
		Mellow Marrow	30							✓				
		Bolón de Verde	32							✓		✓		
	Egg-Based	Breakfast Egg Sandwich	36		✓				✓	✓				
		Breakfast Porridge	38		✓	✓			✓	✓				
		Zucchini Fritters	40		✓									
		Avocado & Egg Salad	42		✓				✓	✓				
		Eggs Benedict	44		✓									
		Eggs Over Raccourci Ratatouille	46		✓			✓	✓	✓				
		Banana Pancakes	48		✓						✓			
		Sweet Potato Breakfast Cookies	50		✓	✓	✓		✓		✓	✓	✓	
		Banana and Carrot Breakfast Cookies *(variation)*	50		✓	✓	✓				✓		✓	
		Nut-Free Breakfast Cookies *(variation)*	50		✓	✓			✓		✓	✓	✓	
Snacks, Appetizers and Side Dishes	Savory	Potage du Jardin	54	✓										
		Cauli-Bread	56		✓				✓	✓				
		Cauli-Pop	58						✓	✓				
		Chic Hummus	60						✓	✓				✓
		Veggie Chips	62	✓										
		Scrambled Coconut Eggs	64		✓	✓								
		Faux Muffins	66		✓									
		Roasted Bone Marrow	68	✓										
		Nori Chips	70											✓
		Clean jerky	72	✓										
		Liver Pâté *(variation)*	120						✓					✓
		Fried Plantain Chips *(variation)*	32							✓		✓		
	Sweet (but sugar-free!)	Cinnamon Ghee Bites	76	✓										
		Coconut MCT Balls	78			✓								
		MCT Bomb Smoothie	80			✓					✓			
		Creamy Popsicles	82			✓					✓			
		Coconut Bark	84			✓	✓				✓			
		Tummy Gummies	86								✓			✓
		Banana Muffins	88		✓	✓					✓			✓
		Muffin *Libre* (egg-free variation)	90			✓					✓			✓
		Fruit Dip *(variation)*	168			✓	✓				✓			
		Creamy Ghee	164	✓										
		Coconut Yogurt	214			✓								✓

| | | | | | | | As Tolerated | | | | | |
Recipes	page	Elimination Phase	Eggs	Coconut	Nuts	Nightshades	FODMAPs	New veggies	Fruits	Starch	Sugar	Other
Main Meals — Chicken												
Golden Chicken	94	✓										
Lemon and Thyme Roasted Chicken	96	✓										
Surprise Chicken Salad	98		✓									✓
Red Meat												
Grass-Fed Steak	102	✓										
Divine Meatballs	104						✓	✓				✓
Asian Meatballs (variation)	104			✓	✓		✓	✓				✓
Mediterranean Burgers	106	✓										
Anticuchos	108						✓					✓
Grass-Fed Steak Tartare	110		✓									
Daylight Pasta	112						✓	✓				
Fajitas de Lengua	114	✓										
Honey & Garlic Ribs	116						✓					✓
Two Shakes of a Lamb's Tail Stew	118	✓										
Bison Multivitamin	120	✓										
Fish												
Grain-Free Sushi	124						✓	✓				✓
Ceviche	126	✓										
Grilled Lemon and Herb Salmon	128	✓										
Omega Boost Salad	130	✓										
Quick Salmon Salad (variation)	130		✓				✓	✓				
Variable Protein												
Speedy Recovery Soup	134	✓										
Speedy Recovery Stew (variation)	134	✓										
Grain-Free Pizza	136		✓				✓	✓				
Naked Wraps	138		✓				✓	✓				✓
Asian Noodle Bowl	140			✓	✓							✓
Aguacate Relleno	142		✓				✓	✓				
Dreamy Creamy Pasta	144						✓	✓				
Double GF Spaghetti	146					✓	✓	✓				
Lasachini	148						✓	✓				
Flavor Boosters												
Caramelized Onions	152						✓					
Chimichurri	154	✓										
Caramelized Garlic	156						✓					
Herbed Ghee	158	✓										
Crock-Pot Ghee	160	✓										
Garlicky Ghee	162	✓										
Coconut Ghee (variation)	160	✓										
Creamy Ghee	164	✓										
Guacamole	166						✓	✓				
Coconut-Asian Sauce	168			✓	✓							✓
Coconut-Asian Sauce (nut-free variation)	168			✓								
Creamy Salad Dressing	98		✓									
Bacon Nest	98											✓
Hollandaise Sauce	170		✓									

Recipes	page	Elimination Phase	Eggs	Coconut	Nuts	Nightshades	FODMAPs	New veggies	Fruits	Starch	Sugar	Other
Flavor Boosters												
Avocado Dressing	144											
Raccourci Ratatouille	172					✓	✓	✓				
Grass-Fed Tallow	174	✓										
Roasted Bone Broth	176	✓										
Herb-Infused Oil	178	✓										
Treats												
Meringue Cookies	182		✓									
Creamy Cream-Free Ice Cream	184			✓			✓		✓			
Banacado	186						✓	✓	✓			
Baked Pear	188			✓			✓		✓			
Grilled Fruit Kebabs	190								✓			
Coconut Whipped Cream	192			✓								
Coconut Fudge	194			✓								
Against-the-Grain Cookies (coconut flour)	196		✓	✓								✓
Against-the-Grain Cookies (almond flour)	196		✓		✓							✓
Crème Brûlée	198		✓	✓							✓	
Mendiants	200			✓	✓				✓			✓
Clean Chocolate Bars (variation)	200			✓								✓
Chocolate Cups (variation)	200											✓
Watermelon Snow	202						✓		✓			
Chocolate Spread (variation)	224			✓							✓	✓
Drinks												
Good-for-the-Tummy Tea	206			✓							✓	✓
Energy Tea Latte	208	✓										
Creamy Chai Energy Tea Latte (variation)	208			✓								✓
Virgin Cocktail	210											✓
Kombucha	218											✓
Roasted Bone Broth	176	✓										
Watermelon Slush (variation)	202						✓		✓			
Ferments												
Coconut Yogurt	214			✓								✓
Coconut Yogurt Gummies (variation)	214			✓								✓
Coconut Cottage (variation)	214			✓								✓
Fermented Pickles	216							✓				✓
Low-Sugar Kombucha	218										✓	✓
Special Projects												
Homemade Coconut Butter	224			✓								
Homemade Coconut Milk	226			✓								
Indoor Herb Garden	228	✓										
Preserve Your Herbs	228	✓										
Frozen Liver Supplements	230	✓										
Activated Nuts	232				✓							
Grow Your Own SCOBY	222										✓	✓

As Tolerated (column group header spanning Eggs through Other)

Breakfasts: Egg-Free

Bananoatmeal / contains banana, coconut and/or nuts

Do you miss your morning bowl of oatmeal? Grains, even gluten-free oats, can be hard to digest or trigger food reactions. Instead, try this no-bake, grain- and gluten-free version using only easy-to-digest REAL food ingredients.

Yields 1 serving:		
1	Banana, ripe	1
2 Tbsp	Coconut butter (or almond butter)	30 ml
Dash	Unrefined salt	Dash
To taste	Cinnamon, berries, unsweetened dried coconut, or nuts (optional)	To taste

1. In a bowl, mash the ripe banana until you obtain a purée. You can also use a blender or food processor.
2. Add the other ingredients and mix.
3. Eat at room temperature or heat for a few seconds in the microwave or in a small saucepan if desired.

TIPS:

- Add coconut milk or homemade yogurt to your grain-free bananoatmeal, as tolerated.
- For **pumpkin or butternut "oatmeal,"** replace the banana with 1 cup (250 ml) of cooked pumpkin or butternut squash.
- Coconut butter is sometimes also called coconut cream concentrate or coconut manna. It's not the same thing as coconut oil.

notes:

Mellow Marrow / contains spaghetti squash

If you don't know what to do with the marrow from the bones you use to make your gut-healing Homemade Bone Broth (p. 244 of *DHwRF*), this is the perfect recipe for you. The nutrient density of bone marrow is so precious that it shouldn't be wasted. If you don't feel quite ready to eat bone marrow by itself (recipe, p. 68), using it as a sauce for your spaghetti squash will help disguise it. This is my favorite breakfast! I enjoy the creaminess of the bone marrow and the fact that the perfect combination of healthy carbs, protein and fats sustains me for hours.

Yields 1 serving:		
1-2 cups	Cooked spaghetti squash	250-500 ml
¼ - ½ cup	Cooked bone marrow (from 1-2 bones)	60-125 ml
¼ - ½ cup	Spinach	60-125 ml
To taste	Seasonings (salt and basil)	To taste

1. To cook the spaghetti squash, cut it in half lengthwise and place it on a lined baking sheet. Bake for about 40-45 minutes or until you can insert a fork easily.
2. Let cool down 10-15 minutes before shredding the flesh of the squash with a fork.
3. Extract the bone marrow from your bones using a knife (this is easier to do after you've boiled your bones for a few hours to make your homemade bone broth). Add it to the warm spaghetti squash and let it melt (if it's cold from being refrigerated).
4. Add a handful of spinach and season to taste.
5. Enjoy!

TIPS:

- If you don't tolerate spaghetti squash, you can always use any other type of vegetables as a support of this dish. Spriralized vegetables (see p. 112) like zucchini, sweet potatoes and carrots would be good substitute for this recipe.
- You can also mix any leftover cooked vegetables with your bone marrow for an even more satisfying, filling breakfast (or as a snack or meal any time of the day).

notes:

Bolón de Verde / contains plantains

Bolón de verde could be described simply as plantain balls. They make a very simple and tasty breakfast, snack or meal anytime of the day. This traditional Ecuadorian recipe is most commonly consumed for breakfast with fried eggs. If you've never cooked plantains (a type of starchy cooking banana), this is the perfect way to get started. And make sure you experiment with different fillings and seasonings to create your own spins on this basic recipe!

Yields 1-2 servings:		
2	Plantains, green	2
¼ cup	Ghee, coconut oil or butter	60 ml
½ cup	Optional meat (chicken, pork or beef)	125 ml
To taste	Seasonings (salt, pepper, cumin, etc.)	To taste

1. Peel the plantains and slice them (about ½ in or 1 cm thick).
2. In a skillet, heat 2 Tbsp (30 ml) of ghee, coconut oil or butter.
3. When melted, add the plantain slices and cook about 15-20 minutes on medium until cooked, stirring every few minutes to ensure that the plantain slices are golden on all sides. If you prefer, you can skip steps 2 and 3 and boil the plantain chunks until soft instead.
4. Transfer to a large bowl and let cool for a few minutes.
5. Mash the cooked plantain slices to obtain a paste. Add seasonings as desired.
6. With your hands, form 6-8 balls with the mashed plantains.
7. If you want, you can form a little hole in the middle of each plantain ball to insert the optional meat (or cheese). Work the mashed plantain around the hole you created to completely hide the filling inside each bolón.
8. In a skillet, heat the remaining 2 Tbsp (30 ml) of fat and fry your bolon de verde a few minutes until warm and golden. Serve immediately.

TIPS:

- Make a big batch in advance and freeze after step 7. Whenever you want a quick breakfast, snack or meal, just thaw a few and fry them up as described in step 8 before serving.
- **Fried plantain chips**. Another good way to enjoy plantains is to cut one or two peeled green plantains into thin slices and fry them in a 2-4 Tbsp (30-60 ml) of coconut oil, Ghee (recipe, p. 160) or Grass-Fed Tallow (recipe, p. 174) for about 4-5 minutes on each side until golden. Sprinkle with a bit of salt and add other seasonings to taste.

Breakfasts: Egg-Based

Breakfast Egg Sandwich / contains FODMAPs (cauliflower) and eggs

The only drawback to eating REAL food is that it's sometimes not as convenient to grab on the go. Not without a container and some cutlery, anyway. This breakfast sandwich uses grain-free cauli-bread to hold all the ingredients of your breakfast so you can start your day with REAL food—even in a hurry. If you expect to be short on time in the morning, assemble your breakfast egg sandwich the night before, wrap it tightly in foil, and refrigerate it until ready to eat.

Yields 1 serving:	
2-4	Cooked cauli-buns (using the Cauli-Bread recipe, p. 56)
2-4	Eggs, cooked to your liking (fried, hard-boiled or poached)
A few slices	Ham, prosciutto or cooked bacon
As desired	Lettuce, spinach, tomato slices, etc.
To taste	Seasonings (salt, pepper, herbs, etc.)
To taste	Creamy Salad Dressing (see recipe, p. 98)
To taste	Guacamole (optional; see recipe, p. 166)

1. Prepare your cauli-buns following the recipe on p. 56.
2. Meanwhile, cook your eggs to your liking.
3. Build your breakfast sandwich with the desired ingredients.
4. Enjoy warm or cold!

TIPS:

- You can prepare a big batch of the cauli-bread recipe in advance. Shape the dough as buns on the lined baking sheet and cook until golden. Once cooled, your cauli-buns can be stored in the freezer for months at a time. Simply put them in a hermetic container with small pieces of parchment paper in between to make them easier to thaw one at a time for an easy breakfast.
- You can also pack this breakfast sandwich to bring as a lunch to work or school. Or eat it as a snack anytime you like!

notes:

Breakfast Porridge / contains FODMAPs (cauliflower), coconut and eggs

If you want a change from the bananoatmeal (recipe, p. 28), or don't tolerate bananas, experiment with this grain-free breakfast porridge. Have it for breakfast or as a snack whenever you want. This porridge provides a great combination of vegetables, healthy fats and protein. It may sound weird to have cauliflower in your porridge, but its bland taste actually provides a great base for the other ingredients.

Yields 1-2 servings:		
1 cup	Cauliflower, grated	250 ml
¼-½ cup	Coconut milk	60-125 ml
½-¾ cup	Water	125-180 ml
2	Eggs, beaten	2
Dash	Unrefined salt	Dash
To taste	Cinnamon, berries, or nuts (optional)	To taste

1. Add the raw grated cauliflower, coconut milk and water to a small saucepan.
2. Bring to a boil and simmer about 8-10 minutes, or until the cauliflower is tender.
3. Add the beaten eggs, whisk and cook 2 more minutes (until the eggs are set).
4. Add your desired seasonings to taste.
5. Serve!

TIPS:

- Vary the proportions of water and coconut milk to get the consistency and taste just right for you.
- **Coconut-free version.** If you don't do well with coconut, simply use water for the liquid part of your porridge and add 1-2 Tbsp (15-30 ml) of ghee, butter or nut butter to add a bit of extra creaminess.
- The fastest way to grate cauliflower is with your food processor or blender. Instead of grating the raw cauliflower by hand, put cauliflower florets in a food processor or blender, cover with water and blend until you obtain small, rice-like chunks of cauliflower.

notes:

Zucchini Fritters / contains eggs

Enjoy these zucchini fritters by themselves or topped with fried eggs for a fun, protein-rich breakfast. You can also add variety to your diet by making these fritters with any other grated vegetables, such as sweet potatoes, carrots, butternut squash, jicama or parsnips (or any combination of the above).

Yields 4 servings:		
1-2 Tbsp	Tallow (recipe, p. 174, or use ghee or coconut oil)	15-30 ml
2	Zucchinis, medium	2
2	Eggs	2
1 Tbsp	Coconut flour (optional)	15 ml
½	Onion, diced (optional)	½
To taste	Unrefined salt and seasonings	To taste

1. Grate the zucchinis and put them in a large bowl.
2. Add the eggs, coconut flour and seasoning to taste. Mix well.
3. In a skillet, heat the tallow. Add about a quarter of the fritter mixture. Cook for a few minutes or until the bottom is cooked. Flip and cook 1-2 minutes on the other side until set.
4. Repeat with the rest of the batch.
5. Serve warm or cold with your desired toppings.

TIPS:

- These fritters can be served as a sweet dish if you prepare them without the onion (with fruits, coconut milk and a bit of maple syrup or honey as tolerated) or as a savory dish (with fried eggs, cooked ground meat, cooked chicken, vegetables, and butter, as tolerated).
- If you have leftovers, they will keep in the fridge for a few days. You can also freeze them, separated with parchment paper to prevent them from sticking together, to have a handy snack option whenever needed.

notes:

Avocado & Egg Salad / contains eggs and FODMAPs (avocado)

This is a quick and easy breakfast, lunch or snack that is very nutrient-dense. The egg yolks provide choline and eye-protecting antioxidants, while the avocado and olive oil provide vitamin E and a sustained source of energy from their healthy fats. This dish also looks quite elegant on a plate! You could even serve it in a Bacon or Prosciutto Nest (recipe, p. 98) for a Sunday special.

Yields 1 serving:		
2-4	Eggs, hard-boiled	2-4
½-1	Avocado, ripe	½-1
1-2 Tbsp	Extra-virgin olive oil	15-30 ml
1-2 Tbsp	Lemon juice	15-30 ml
To taste	Unrefined salt and seasonings	To taste

1. Peel your hard-boiled eggs. Cut them in half and cut each half into quarters.
2. Peel and cut your half or whole avocado into cubes.
3. Mix the eggs and avocado in a bowl.
4. Drizzle with the olive oil and lemon juice. Season to taste, and mix.
5. Serve immediately (otherwise the avocado may start browning)!

TIPS:

- **Creamy version**. Replace the oil and lemon juice with the Creamy Salad Dressing (recipe, p. 98).
- Boil your large eggs about 4-5 minutes if you like the yolk runny or about 6 minutes if you prefer it fully cooked.
- If you pack this salad in your lunch, the avocado may brown a little. Add a bit more lemon juice to prevent oxidation. Browned avocado is not dangerous to consume, and you can just scrape it to make your salad look pretty again.

notes:

Eggs Benedict / contains eggs

This fancy breakfast can be made grain-free without any problems. Be creative with the different bases and toppings for this recipe until you come up with your own Eggs Benedict specialty! You can serve this elegant dish any time of the day.

Yields 1-2 servings:		Special tips
Base	Portobello mushroom caps	Grill the mushroom caps at 375°F (190°C) on a baking pan for about 15 minutes or until soft.
	Cauli-buns	Follow the recipe for making cauliflower dough on p. 56, but shape the dough into buns to make grain-free and gluten-free English muffins.
	Bacon Nest	Follow recipe on p. 98.
	Prosciutto or ham slices	No preparation needed.
	Tomato slices	Simply slice your tomato. You can leave it raw or grill the slices in the oven for a few minutes.
	Grilled eggplant slices	Grill the eggplant slices at 375°F (190°C) drizzled with olive oil on a baking pan for about 20-25 minutes or until soft.
	Sweet potato slices	Cook the sweet potato slices at 375°F (190°C) drizzled with coconut oil or ghee on a baking pan for about 20-25 minutes or until soft.
	Zucchini Fritters	Follow recipe on p. 40.
Eggs	Fresh eggs, ideally pastured	
Sauce	Hollandaise sauce (recipe, p. 170)	
Toppings	Bacon slices, prosciutto or ham, avocado slices, sautéed mushrooms, spinach or kale, asparagus Seasonings (salt, pepper, herbs, green onions, etc.)	

1. Prepare the base first by following the tips in the table above.
2. In the meantime, bring a large pot of water to a boil. You can also add 1-2 tsp (5-10 ml) of white vinegar to the water to make the poaching of your eggs easier. Once boiling, turn off the heat to keep your water simmering gently.
3. Crack your eggs (not too many at once for best results) in the simmering water.
4. Let cook for about 3 minutes if you want the yolk runny to about 5 minutes if you want it cooked.
5. Carefully remove the eggs with a slotted spoon and place on a paper towel to dry the excess water.
6. Prepare the hollandaise sauce following the recipe on p. 170.
7. On a plate, layer the base, the poached eggs, and the desired toppings, and drizzle with the Hollandaise sauce.

TIPS:

- Remember to only use ingredients you know you tolerate well. Avoid tomato and eggplant if you're sensitive to nightshades and stay away from mushrooms, cauliflower, asparagus and avocado if FODMAPs are a trigger for you.
- Adding 1 tsp (5 ml) of vinegar to the boiling water can make the poaching process easier by helping the eggs hold together better.

Eggs over Raccourci Ratatouille

/ contains eggs, FODMAPs and nightshades

If you're in a rut with your egg-based breakfast, try serving your eggs over this easy ratatouille sauce for a change.

Yields 1 serving:		
1-2 cups	Raccourci Ratatouille (recipe, p. 172)	250-500 ml
2-4	Eggs	2-4
1-2 Tbsp	Ghee, coconut oil or tallow	15-30 ml
To taste	Unrefined salt and seasonings	To taste

1. In a skillet, heat your desired fat and fry your eggs to your liking. Season to taste.
2. In the meantime, heat your ready-to-eat raccourci ratatouille.
3. Serve your fried eggs over the warm ratatouille. Bon appétit!

TIPS:

- Poached eggs with a runny egg yolk work well with this recipe too.
- Add avocado slices if desired.
- Sprinkle with cheese if you tolerate dairy.

notes:

Banana Pancakes / contains banana and eggs

Most grain-free pancake recipes use either coconut flour or almond flour, but this recipe uses none. The only two ingredients you require are bananas and eggs. If your digestive system doesn't do well with banana, you can substitute them with the same amount of puréed butternut squash or unsweetened applesauce.

Yields about 4-6 pancakes (about 6 in or 15 cm in diameter):			
Basic	2 Tbsp 3 large 1 cup	Coconut oil, ghee, butter or tallow Eggs Bananas (2 to 4 depending on the size)	30 ml 4 medium 250 ml
Optional	½ cup 2 Tbsp 1 tsp 2 Tbsp	Unsweetened dried coconut Unsweetened cocoa powder Cinnamon Nuts and/or dried fruits	125 ml 30 ml 5 ml 30 ml

1. Mash the bananas and mix them with the beaten eggs. You can also use a blender or food processor.
2. In a skillet, heat your chosen fat until melted. Make sure the skillet is hot enough before moving to step 3, otherwise the batter will be soggy and hard to flip.
3. Scoop about ¼ cup (60 ml) of batter into the skillet and cook on medium for 3-4 minutes, or until you see little holes appear on the uncooked side of your pancake.
4. Flip and cook for an additional 2-3 minutes.
5. Repeat with the rest of the batter.
6. Serve warm. Top with butter, ghee, coconut milk, homemade plain yogurt (see Coconut Yogurt recipe, p. 214), fresh fruits, nut butter, honey, maple syrup or melted dark chocolate if desired.

TIPS:

- You can also make a larger batch of these banana pancakes and cook them in advance. Keep the cooked pancakes in the fridge (for 2-3 days) or in the freezer (for 3-6 months). Simply reheat whenever you want
- You can decrease the ratio of fruit sugar and increase the proportion of protein in this recipe by mixing an egg per half banana (instead of about an egg per banana). The texture will be a bit more omelet-like, but still very satisfying, especially served with generous amounts of ghee, butter or coconut oil.
- If you don't like the sweeter taste of bananas, substitute with the same quantity of green plantains.

Sweet Potato Breakfast Cookies

/ contains FODMAPs and starches (sweet potatoes), eggs, coconut, nuts and sugar

Tired of eating meat or eggs for breakfast? These breakfast cookies are super convenient and packed with healthy fats. Although this recipe includes starches and nuts, you can use nut-free and starch-free ingredient substitutions (see tip section). This recipe is quite forgiving, so don't be afraid to play with the ingredients to create your own customized version with ingredients you enjoy (and tolerate). If you don't tolerate eggs, use the Muffin Libre (p. 90) to make your egg-free breakfast cookies.

Yields 18 medium breakfast cookies (6-9 breakfasts):		
3 cups	Sweet potatoes, cooked and puréed (about 3 small)	750 ml
1/3 cup	Coconut flour	80 ml
1 cup	Shredded coconut, unsweetened	250 ml
½ cup	Almond butter	125 ml
¼ cup	Coconut sugar, honey or maple syrup (optional)	60 ml
5	Eggs, large	5
¼ cup	Ghee, butter, coconut oil or cocoa butter	60 ml
1 cup	Dark chocolate, nuts and/or dried fruits (optional)	250 ml
To taste	Dash of salt, cinnamon, grated ginger, nutmeg, etc.	To taste

1. Prepare the sweet potato purée by boiling peeled, chopped sweet potatoes for 20-25 minutes, until easy to pierce with a fork. Remove the cooked sweet potatoes and let cool down on a plate. Mash or purée the sweet potatoes until you obtain a smooth consistency.
2. Add all the ingredients and mix until homogenous. You might need to heat the almond butter or ghee before adding them if they are too hard.
3. Spoon the cookie batter on a lined baking sheet.
4. Bake at 350°F (180°C) for about 15-20 minutes or until the edges are golden and the center appears cooked.
5. Enjoy with a glass of coconut milk!

TIPS:

- This is a big batch of cookies. You can easily freeze part of your batch, keeping your cookies from sticking together by placing parchment paper between them.
- This breakfast provides a lot of healthy fat along with a moderate amount of healthy carbs. The protein content is on the low side, so you can either pack some clean jerky (recipe, p. 72) or hard-boiled eggs with your breakfast cookies or eat more protein at the following meals to compensate.
- **Banana version.** If you don't tolerate sweet potatoes (or simply want a different taste), replace the mashed sweet potatoes with mashed bananas.
- **Add vegetables!** You can also replace 1 cup (250 ml) of the sweet potato or banana purée with grated carrots or grated zucchini to add a bit of nutrient-dense vegetables to your breakfast.
- The sugar in this recipe is optional; you can omit it without big changes to the texture.
- **Nut-free version.** If you don't tolerate nuts, you can replace the almond butter with coconut butter (store-bought or homemade as explained on p. 224) or sunflower seed butter. Another alternative is to replace the almond butter with about 1/3 cup (80 ml) of fat (ghee, butter or coconut oil) and add an extra egg or two to give the batter the desired consistency.

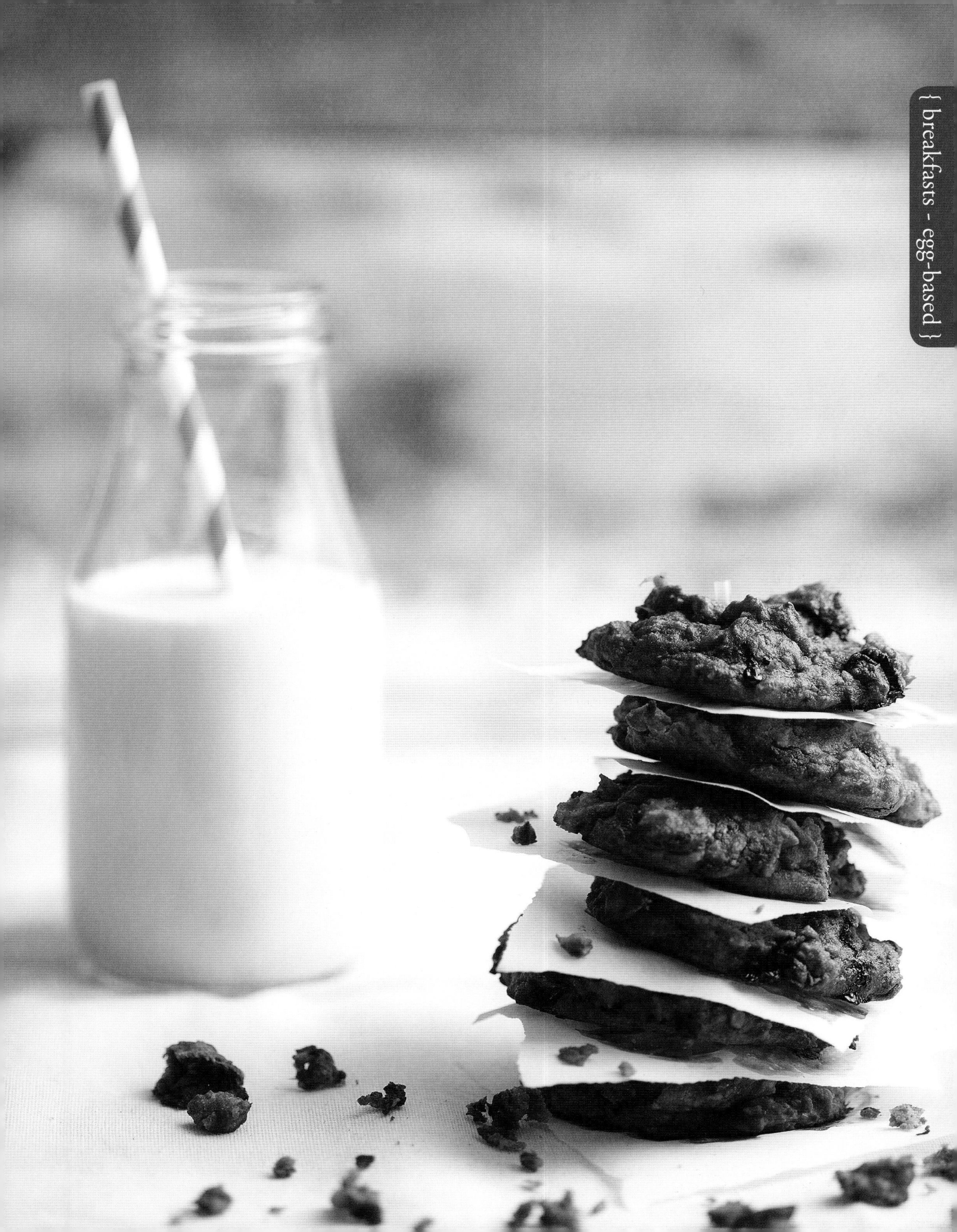

Snack, Appetizers & Side Dishes: Savory

Potage du Jardin / appropriate for the elimination phase

Potages, or blended soups, are a great way to add vegetables to your diet in an easy-to-digest form. You can serve your blended soup as a side dish or add your protein directly to your potage, along with a bit of extra fat if needed, to enjoy a complete and balanced meal that will be easy to digest and gentle on your digestive system. A drizzle of garlic-infused oil (FODMAP-free recipe, p. 284 of *DHwRF*), Garlicky Ghee (recipe, p. 162), ghee or coconut oil can make your blended soup richer and more satisfying.

Yields 4-8 servings:			
Fat	2-4 Tbsp	Ghee, coconut oil or olive oil	30-60 ml
Liquid	4 cups	Homemade bone broth (recipe, p. 176) or water	1 L
Vegetables	4 cups	Any tolerated vegetables, grossly chopped (zucchini, carrots, onions, garlic, tomatoes, winter squash, asparagus, broccoli, cauliflower, etc.)	1 L
Seasonings	To taste	Salt, pepper, herbs and spices	To taste

1. This step is optional, but can enhance the taste of your soup. In a large pot, melt generous amounts of coconut oil or ghee on medium-high and add your vegetables. You don't need to cook them thoroughly at this point; just quickly stir them a few minutes under medium-high heat to get a bit of caramelization or browning and intensify their flavors.
2. Add all the other ingredients (liquid and seasonings). Don't worry too much about the seasonings if you're not sure how much you need. Add a little and you'll be able to adjust the seasonings before serving the soup.
3. Bring your soup to a boil. Once your soup has reached the boiling point, decrease the temperature to the lowest setting allowing it to simmer gently.
4. Let simmer for at least 20-30 minutes to up to 1 hour, or until the vegetables are tender and thoroughly cooked. Harder vegetables like winter squash may need more time than zucchini for example. Use a fork to test if your vegetables are ready. Remove from the heat and let cool down a little.
5. Use a hand blender to reduce your soup into a puree. If you don't have a hand blender, carefully transfer the soup (careful, it's hot!) to a blender or food processor and blend until smooth (you may need to do more than one batch to prevent overflows).
6. Adjust the seasoning and return the blended soup to the pot to keep warm before serving.

TIPS:

- If you want your blended soup thicker, use more vegetables or add about 1-2 Tbsp (15-30 ml) of coconut flour. Start with the smaller amount and wait at least 5 minutes before adding more because it takes some time to thicken up. Mix the coconut flour in a small amount of liquid before adding it to the soup to prevent lumps from forming.
- If your soup is too thick, add more water or bone broth until you get the desired consistency.
- You can always make your soup creamier without dairy by adding ½-1 cup (125-250 ml) of coconut milk (ideally without guar gum or other ingredients). If you tolerate dairy, you can use ½-1 cup (125-250 ml) of cream. Always add the coconut milk or cream after step 8, right before serving.
- Try some of the following combinations of vegetables and seasonings, but don't be afraid to experiment with whatever vegetables and seasonings you have in your kitchen.

Carrot	Zucchini	Butternut Squash	Cauliflower
Add 1-2 tsp (5-10 ml) of cinnamon and a dash of nutmeg, to taste. OR add ½ cup of orange juice, the zest of an orange and 1-2 tsp (5-10 ml) of freshly grated ginger.	Add ¼ tsp (1 ml) of dried thyme, ¼ tsp (1 ml) of dried rosemary and ½ tsp (2 ml) dried basil. Serve with fresh dill. You can also add garlic and onions to the vegetable blend if tolerated.	Add 1-2 Tbsp (15-30 ml) grated ginger and 2 tsp (10 ml) of turmeric. You can also add garlic and onions to the vegetable blend if tolerated.	Use only 2 cups of liquid in the recipe. When the cauliflower is cooked, add 2 cups (500 ml) of coconut milk, 1 tsp (5 ml) turmeric, 1 tsp (5 ml) of freshly grated ginger and the juice of half a lime. You can also add garlic and onions to the vegetable blend if tolerated.

Cauli-Bread / contains FODMAPs (cauliflower) and eggs

You can use a simple mixture of cauliflower and eggs to form a dough and replace old favorites like buns, crackers and pizza dough. Don't expect to get the exact same texture and taste as regular grain-based bread, but this cauli-bread still makes a wonderful base for your REAL food. Use it as a snack, spread it with ghee, butter, or nut butter, or use it to make delicious grain-free sandwiches (recipe, p. 36), burgers (recipe, p. 106) and pizza (recipe, p. 136).

Yields about 4-8 slices of cauli-bread:		
3 cups	Cauliflower, grated	750 ml
2 Tbsp	Coconut oil, ghee or lard	30 ml
3	Eggs, large	3
To taste	Unrefined salt and seasonings (pepper, dried herbs, crushed garlic, etc.)	To taste

1. Whisk the grated cauliflower with the eggs and seasonings until you get a dough-like texture.
2. Drop the cauliflower dough on a lined baking sheet and shape it as desired. You can make round buns, squares, a pizza dough, or any other shape you like.
3. Bake at 400-425°F (200-220°C) for about 10-20 minutes or until the dough is cooked and the edges are slightly golden (the larger and thicker it is, the longer it will take to cook).
4. Let cool down and enjoy!

TIPS:

- Eat this cauli-bread on its own or use it as a base on which to spread your Liver Pâté (beef version, p. 120 of this cookbook or chicken version, p. 294 of *DHwRF*) or nut butter, for example.
- The fastest way to grate cauliflower is with your food processor or blender. Instead of grating the raw cauliflower by hand, put cauliflower florets in a food processor or blender, cover with water and blend until you obtain small, rice-like chunks.

notes:

Cauli-Pop / contains FODMAPs (cauliflower)

Cauliflower is so versatile, and many people can successfully reintroduce it, at least occasionally in small amounts, after the elimination phase of the *DHwRF* protocol. Unfortunately, the same can't be said for corn. Although most people consider it a vegetable, it's actually a grain that shares many of the irritating compounds found in other grains. If you miss popcorn, try this cauli-pop recipe. It doesn't have the same crunch, but its flavor, appearance and nutrition will pop in your mouth without popping later in your intestines.

Yields about 2-3 cups (500-750 ml):		
1 head	Cauliflower	1 head
2-4 Tbsp	Coconut oil, ghee or tallow	30-60 ml
To taste	Seasonings (salt, pepper, onion or garlic powder, dried herbs, etc.)	To taste

1. Cut your cauliflower into small florets, about the size of individual popped popcorn kernels. You can skip the knife and only use your hands for this step to break down the cauliflower head into florets.
2. Place your florets on a lined baking sheet, in a single layer.
3. Drizzle (or spread if solid) your chosen fat on the cauliflower florets and sprinkle with the desired seasonings. To make this step easier, do this step in a bowl. If you want to have one fewer thing to wash, simply mix with your hand directly on the baking sheet.
4. Bake at 400°F (200°C) for about 30-40 minutes, stirring every 5-10 minutes to prevent burning, until golden.
5. Serve hot, warm or cold!

TIPS:

- Turmeric is a great seasoning for this recipe. Try using about 1-3 tsp (5-15 ml), depending on the size of your cauliflower head, to coat your cauli-pop with a yellow color and give it anti-inflammatory superpowers.
- This cauli-pop is great as a snack or as a side dish. Enjoy it without any guilt!

notes:

Chic Hummus / contains FODMAPs (cauliflower) and sesame seeds

What's so chic about this hummus recipe? It's chickpea-free! Although cauliflower contains some FODMAPs, a moderate serving of this chic hummus is less likely to cause you bloating, gas or other inconvenient or uncomfortable symptoms that aren't so chic. Use this hummus to dip your vegetables (raw or cooked), chicken kebabs (recipe, p. 262 of *DHwRF*), Veggie Chips (recipe, p. 62) and Mediterranean Burgers (recipe, p. 106), as a spread for your Naked Wraps (recipe, p. 138) and hard-boiled eggs, or even as a salad dressing.

Yields about 2 cups (500 ml):

1 head	Cauliflower	1 head
2 Tbsp	Coconut oil, ghee or tallow	30 ml
¼ cup	Tahini (sesame seeds paste) or almond butter	60 ml
1 Tbsp	Lemon juice	15 ml
2 Tbsp	Coconut aminos (optional)	30 ml
To taste	Seasonings (salt, pepper, garlic powder, cumin, etc.)	To taste

1. Cut your cauliflower into small florets, about the size of individual popped popcorn kernels. You can skip the knife and only use your hands for this step to break down the cauliflower head into florets.
2. Place your florets on a lined baking sheet, in a single layer.
3. Drizzle (or spread if solid) your chosen fat on the cauliflower florets.
4. Bake at 400°F (200°C) for about 30-40 minutes, stirring every 5-10 minutes to prevent burning, until golden.
5. Let the roasted cauliflower cool for a few minutes.
6. Transfer to a food processor and add all of the other ingredients. Blend until smooth.
7. Transfer your chic hummus to a bowl. Serve right away or refrigerate 2-3 hours until cold before serving for a firmer consistency.

TIPS:

- **Garlic chic hummus.** Give your hummus a garlicky flavor by adding crushed garlic or garlic powder. If you don't tolerate the high-FODMAP content of garlic, simply substitute the fat in this recipe with Garlicky Ghee (recipe, p. 162) for a FODMAP-free version of this garlic chic hummus.
- This Chic Hummus can keep for about 5 days in the fridge.
- If you're in a rush, you can simply boil your cauliflower before moving to step 6.

Veggie Chips / appropriate for the elimination phase

Homemade veggie chips make the perfect grain-free complement for many REAL food-based snacks. They work great on their own or as a cracker spread with Liver Pâté (beef version, p. 120 of this cookbook or chicken version, p. 294 of *DHwRF*) or Roasted Bone Marrow (recipe, p. 68). Try using different vegetables like zucchini, eggplant or sweet potatoes—the possibilities are endless if you want to find new ways to satisfy your cravings for something crunchy!

Yields about 2 cups (500 ml):		
2 cups	Vegetables (zucchini or carrots)	2 medium (500 m)
3-4 Tbsp	Olive oil	45-60 ml
To taste	Unrefined salt and seasonings	To taste

1. Wash your chosen vegetables and slice them thinly to form chips or crackers.
2. Put the slices on a lined baking sheet. You will probably need at least two. If you have only one, do one batch at a time and repeat the steps until you're done.
3. Drizzle with generous amounts of olive oil and sprinkle with salt.
4. Bake in the oven at 275°F (135°C), turning every 15 minutes or so, for a total of about 45 minutes until dried and crisp. The amount of time required for your veggie chips to be ready depends on the type of vegetable you choose and the thickness of the slices. The taste test is the best way to confirm they're ready!

TIPS:

- After the elimination phase, you can experiment with more vegetables like butternut squash, kale, eggplant (nightshade), beets, plantain, sweet potatoes, etc.
- You can also use a food dehydrator if you have one. It should take around 6-10 hours depending on the thickness of your chips, or until the veggie chips are crispy to your liking. You can use raw slices of vegetables, but I prefer the flavor when I cook them prior to dehydrating them. It's easier to slice the vegetables into chips (with the exception of kale, of course) before cooking them by boiling or grilling in the oven drizzled with fat.

notes:

Scrambled Coconut Eggs / contains eggs and coconut

Eggs are versatile and can be combined with almost any ingredient you tolerate to create something new and tasty. Unsweetened dried coconut is an easy way to make your eggs more interesting while adding more healthy fats. Dried coconut, even if unsweetened, also has a naturally sweet taste that can help satisfy your sweet tooth.

Yields 1 serving:			
Basic	1-2 Tbsp 2-4 2-4 Tbsp	Coconut oil or ghee Eggs, beaten Unsweetened dried shredded coconut	15-30 ml 2-4 30-60 ml
Make It a Meal!	½-1 cup 1-2 oz	Vegetables Chicken, cooked	125-250 ml 30-60 g

1. Heat the coconut oil in a skillet.
2. Add the eggs and unsweetened dried coconut.
3. Add the vegetables and cooked chicken if desired.
4. Use a wooden spoon to mix and fold the eggs as they cook.
5. Once you get the right consistency, turn off the heat and serve.

TIPS:

- Add spinach, mushroom and cooked chicken, then scramble your eggs with the unsweetened dried coconut for a delicious meal.
- You can add a splash of coconut milk to make your scrambled coconut eggs even creamier.
- You can enhance the coconut flavor in the recipe by first grilling the shredded coconut in a non-adhesive skillet under medium heat for a few minutes, stirring regularly to prevent burning, until slightly golden.

notes:

Faux Muffins / contains eggs

These faux muffins make a quick and easy snack to bring with you. These "muffins" are 100 percent grain-free and sugar-free. Try different combinations of vegetables and seasonings to create interesting variations. You can make ginger and broccoli faux muffins, spinach, sun-dried tomatoes, basil and Parmesan faux muffins or mushroom, onion, sausage, thyme and rosemary faux muffins. Be creative!

Yields 12 faux muffins:		
4-6	Eggs	4-6
1 cup	Vegetables of your choice	250 ml
1-2 Tbsp	Coconut oil or ghee	15-30 ml
To taste	Unrefined salt and seasonings	To taste

1. Slice or cut your vegetables into small pieces, or grate them if you prefer.
2. Heat the fat in a skillet and add the vegetables. Cook for 5-10 minutes or until tender. You can skip this step if you don't mind the vegetables al dente.
3. Meanwhile, beat the eggs in a large bowl. Add the cooked vegetables and season to taste.
4. Pour the omelet mixture in a muffin tin greased with coconut oil or use individual silicone muffin cups.
5. Bake in the oven at 350°F (180°C) for about 20 minutes or until the center is set.
6. Enjoy cold or warm.

TIPS:

- Add pieces of bacon, cooked sausage, or cheese (if tolerated).
- These faux muffins can keep for 4-5 days in the fridge. You can also make an extra large batch and freeze extras for a quick breakfast or snack on the go.
- If you have these faux muffins for breakfast, make sure you eat enough of them to get the equivalent of at least 2-3 eggs, or combine your faux muffins with sausages or leftover meat and vegetables for a complete meal.

notes:

Roasted Bone Marrow / appropriate for the elimination phase

Bone marrow is one of the most nutritious parts of the animal, and it's no surprise that our ancestors worked hard to find ways to access this nutritional treasure. There was a time where humans kept the marrow and organ meat for themselves and fed the muscle meat to their dogs. We seem to have lost this nutritional wisdom in recent decades, but it's not too late to reverse bad habits. Discover the nutty taste and creamy texture of bone marrow while benefiting from its healthy fats and fat-soluble nutrients.

Yields 3-4 servings:		
1-2 lb	Beef bones with marrow	0.5-1 kg

1. Preheat the oven at 450°F (230°C).
2. Line a baking sheet with parchment paper or aluminum foil.
3. Place your bones perpendicularly on the baking sheet so the bone marrow is exposed at the top.
4. Sprinkle with salt, pepper and herbs if desired.
5. Roast for about 15-20 minutes depending on the thickness of your bones.
6. Let cool the bones a few minutes before serving (otherwise you'll burn yourself!).
7. Eat by scooping out the bone marrow.

TIPS:

- Use the oil that drips at the bottom of the pan for cooking vegetables (or drizzling it on top).
- You can also spread your bone marrow on your Veggie Chips (recipe, p. 62), or try the Mellow Marrow (recipe, p. 30).
- If you enjoy your roasted bone marrow the first time you make it, add a bone marrow spoon to your wish list to make it easier to eat the next time around. ;)
- Ask your butcher to cut your marrow bones lengthwise to make the roasting process easier.
- Use the roasted bones to make Homemade Bone Broth (recipe, p. 176).

notes:

Nori Chips / contains seaweed

These nori chips are perfect if you're looking for a little crunchy snack to nibble on. You might be able to find similar versions in health food stores, but they usually come with a high price tag. In addition, they often contain added sugar, inflammatory rancid vegetable oils, and nightshade-derived seasonings (such as chili or paprika) that may not be right for you. Make a few batches of nori chips at once—they keep at room temperature forever and can help satisfy your cravings whenever temptation hits.

Yields 24 Nori Chips:		
4 1-2 Tbsp To taste	Nori sheets Olive oil, coconut oil or sesame oil (or a mix of these oils) Seasonings (salt, pepper, dried herbs, sesame seeds, coconut aminos, gluten-free tamari sauce, garlic powder, chili powder, etc.)	4 15-30 ml To taste

1. Place the nori sheets on a cutting board and cut them, using a sharp knife, into 6 pieces. You can have fun with this part and try to shape your nori sheets any way you like (clean scissors make it easier).
2. Transfer the nori sheets on a lined baking sheet.
3. Use a brush (or your fingers) to spread a thin layer of olive oil on your nori sheets.
4. Sprinkle with the desired seasonings.
5. Bake for about 20 minutes, turning them once if needed, at 250°F (120°C) until crisp.
6. Let cool down and transfer to a hermetic container or bag.
7. Enjoy!

TIPS:

- Nori and seaweed are great sources of iodine, a mineral that might be hard to get if you're avoiding table (iodized) salt.
- Serve these nori chips at your next party! Not only is nori tasty, but it's also healthy and good for your tummy.
- Use your dehydrator instead of the oven if you prefer.

notes:

Clean Jerky / appropriate for the elimination phase

Jerky makes a perfect on-the-go snack, even for the first phase of your elimination diet. But you have to make it yourself. The problem with commercial jerky is that it is usually made using low-quality meat, it is commonly added with problematic ingredients like gluten, soy, MSG or chili (a nightshade) and it often comes with a high price tag. Although you'll first need to invest in a food dehydrator to make this recipe, making your own homemade clean jerky from ground beef will help you save money in the long run in addition to giving you a very convenient and clean source of protein.

Yields 10-20 servings of about 12-25 g of protein each:		
2 lb	Ground beef, ideally grass-fed	900 g
2 tsp	Salt	10 ml
To taste	Seasonings (black pepper, dried herbs, etc.)	To taste

1. In a large bowl, mix the ground beef with salt and other seasonings to taste.
2. On a large surface area, place a rectangle of parchment paper where you can place about half of the seasoned ground beef.
3. Line with another layer of parchment paper and roll with a rolling pin until you obtain a thin layer (about ¼-1/8 in or 0.5-1 cm thick).
4. Using a pizza cutter (make sure it has been cleaned thoroughly if you are sensitive to gluten), cut slices of ground meat of about 4 in x 1 in (10 cm x 2 cm), although the exact size doesn't really matter.
5. Place the slices of ground beef on your dehydrator tray. Repeat steps 2-4 until you've used all the meat.
6. Let the meat dehydrate for about 10-16 hours (overnight) until it's dehydrated enough that the jerky breaks when trying to bend it.
7. You can store your clean jerky in the fridge or freezer for months. It will also keep for a few weeks at room temperature without any problems, so you can bring some with you when you think you might need a snack or extra protein.

TIPS:

- Be creative with this jerky recipe. You can even add bits of cooked bacon, dried cranberries or nuts.
- **Seasonings**. Vary the seasonings of this recipe. You can add a couple of tablespoons of coconut aminos or balsamic vinegar, a teaspoon of chili peppers or paprika if you tolerate nightshades or a few cloves of crushed garlic if you tolerate FODMAPs. One of my favorite variations to give my jerky an Asian twist consists in adding 2 Tbsp (30 ml) of coconut aminos, 2 tsp (10 ml) of freshly grated ginger and 2 tsp (10 ml) of cooked grated garlic.
- **1 oz = 3 oz!** Although meat shrinks when dehydrated, it doesn't lose any of its nutritional value. The dehydration process gets rid of most of the water and some of the fat but preserves all the nutritious protein and other healthy nutrients. Keep in mind that each ounce (30 g) of your jerky is the equivalent of about 3 oz (90 g) of freshly cooked meat and therefore provides around 25 g of protein.
- You can make jerky with any cuts of meat. All you need to do is slice it very thinly, marinate it if you want to boost its flavor, and dehydrate it following the same instructions. If your meat is frozen, put it in the fridge for a few hours until semi-thawed before slicing it. It's actually easier to slice when still semi-frozen, but you can still do it if the meat is completely thawed. Then simply marinate the sliced meat in balsamic vinegar or coconut aminos and your favorite seasonings, ideally overnight. I even make jerky with leftovers from the Anticuchos (recipe, p. 108) and it's delicious!

Snack, Appetizers & Side Dishes: Sweet

Cinnamon Ghee Bites / appropriate for the elimination phase

These frozen cinnamon ghee bites are wonderful to curb cravings and provide a quick energy boost. Fat is filling and full of nutrients, and it can help stabilize your energy levels for longer than any other macronutrient.

Yields about 15 bites:		
½ lb	Ghee, room temperature	225 g
½ Tbsp	Cinnamon	8 ml
½ tsp	Vanilla	2 ml

1. Mix all the ingredients in a food processor. You can also use Creamy Ghee (recipe, p. 164) for creamier cinnamon ghee bites.
2. Drop the cinnamon and ghee mixture into dollops on a lined baking sheet.
3. Freeze for about an hour or until set.
4. Transfer to a hermetic container and keep frozen.
5. Enjoy whenever you need a treat or to fight off a craving.

TIPS:

- Add a bit of honey or maple syrup to the mixture before freezing if tolerated.
- A tablespoon or two (15-30 ml) of finely grated carrots also works very well with this recipe (cook the carrots beforehand if you don't tolerate raw vegetables very well). It's almost like carrot cake!

notes:

Coconut MCT balls / contains coconut

Disclaimer: These dairy-free, grain-free, gluten-free, egg-free balls may be highly addictive! In addition to their candy-like taste, these coconut balls have a very high medium-chain triglyceride (MCT) content. MCT is a very special type of fat found almost exclusively in coconut. All natural fats are good, but MCT fats have special powers: they give you a quick boost of energy, and they have antimicrobial properties. If you're worried about your weight, MCT fats are a good option because they can't really be stored in your body, unlike other fats. These coconut MCT balls are therefore the perfect snack to keep you going between your meals. They make also a satisfying treat to satisfy your sweet tooth without taking your blood sugar (and energy levels) on a roller coaster ride.

Yields about 12 coconut MCT balls:		
½ cup	Coconut butter	125 ml
½ cup	Unsweetened dried shredded coconut	125 ml
1 Tbsp	Water	15 ml
To taste	Vanilla extract	To taste

1. Mix all the ingredients together in a large bowl.
2. Form balls using about 1-2 Tbsp (15-30 ml) of the mixture. If the mixture is too runny, refrigerate it for 15-30 minutes.
3. Place the coconut balls on a lined baking sheet.
4. Choose one of these three ways to complete your coconut MCT balls recipe (try each one to see which you like better):

   - Your coconut MCT balls are already ready! Leave them at room temperature and eat.
   - Refrigerate your coconut MCT balls for at least 30-60 minutes if you want a firmer texture.
   - Bake your coconut MCT balls at 350°F (180°C) for about 20 minutes or until the coconut balls become fragrant and slightly golden. Let cool before popping one in your mouth if you don't want to burn yourself (speaking from experience!). Baking your coconut MCT balls crisps them up a little and deepens the flavor. This is usually my favorite method.

TIPS:

- Coconut butter is sometimes also called coconut cream concentrate or coconut manna. It is not the same as coconut oil. When you open your jar of coconut butter, it's possible that a layer of coconut oil has formed on top of it. Put the jar in a large bowl and fill it with hot water. Let rest a few minutes until the coconut butter softens and mix until homogenous. This is important, as not doing so could change the outcome of this recipe.
- These coconut MCT balls can be kept at room temperature for many days without any problems. They can also last even longer in the fridge or freezer. Double or triple the batch if you want to keep some on hand in your freezer (they thaw very quickly).
- **Add flavors!** As you tolerate more ingredients, add dried fruits, nuts and unsweetened cocoa powder, and sweeten with honey and maple syrup if desired.
- **Apple pie version.** Add grated apples, cinnamon, nutmeg and roasted walnuts for a nice apple pie flavor.

MCT Bomb Smoothie / contains coconut milk and fruits

If you want to take a break from eating meat and vegetables for breakfast or another meal, try making this dairy-free smoothie a few days a week to switch things up. You can also have it as a snack or dessert. MCT stands for medium-chain triglycerides, a very unique type of fat found almost exclusively in coconut (other natural sources include palm kernel oil and human milk). MCTs are preferentially burned for energy in your body, and their energizing effect is steadier than that of caffeine. Adding a dose of MCTs to your daily diet can help you maintain higher energy levels for hours.

Yields 1-2 servings:

½ cup	Fruits (banana, berries, mango, peaches, kiwi, etc.)	125 ml
¼ cup	Vegetables (spinach, kale, avocado, cooked pumpkin, etc.)	60 ml
½ - 1 cup	Coconut milk	125 - 250 ml
1-2 Tbsp	Coconut butter (optional)	30-60 ml
To taste	Turmeric, cinnamon, vanilla extract (optional)	To taste

1. Put all the ingredients in a blender, starting with the smaller amount of coconut milk.
2. Blend until smooth. Add more coconut milk if your smoothie is too thick to get the desired consistency (or try coconut water if you don't want your smoothie to be too rich).
3. Blend again to make your smoothie homogenous.
4. Enjoy!

TIPS:

- If you tolerate dairy, use your homemade yogurt instead of the coconut milk.
- Use Coconut Yogurt (recipe, p. 214) in this recipe if you need a boost of gut-friendly bacteria.
- Sweeten with honey and nut butter if tolerated.
- If you don't do too well with fruits, substitute them with puréed carrots, butternut squash or avocado. Sprinkle with cinnamon to taste.
- Avocado makes a great addition to your smoothies, adding healthy fats and making the texture extra creamy.
- You can turn your smoothie super green by adding a bit of liquid chlorophyll to it.
- Refrigerate your coconut milk if you want your smoothie to be cold. Or add a few ice cubes.
- Coconut butter is sometimes also called coconut cream concentrate or coconut manna. It is not the same as coconut oil. There is no problem in adding coconut oil to your MCT Bomb Smoothie but be aware that the cold temperature of the other ingredients usually causes the coconut oil to form unpleasant lumps.
- Add extra protein and gut-healing nutrients to your MCT Bomb Smoothie by sprinkling 1 Tbsp (15 ml) of gelatin (ideally from grass-fed, pastured animals, like the Great Lakes brand) and 500-1,000 mg of L-glutamine powder (or the powder from 1-2 capsules). Just make sure you sprinkle the gelatin in a very thin layer and let it absorb water for a few minutes to avoid lumps. The L-glutamine dissolves very easily, so simply blend until dissolved.

Creamy Popsicles / contains coconut and fruits

Most frozen treats are loaded with sugar and processed ingredients, in addition to gut-irritating gums and thickeners, and they usually contain very little in the way of nutrient-dense REAL food. Make your own popsicles, using only ingredients you tolerate, to enjoy as a dessert or snack anytime of the year.

Yields 4-6 popsicles (depending on the size of your molds):		
1 cup	Coconut milk	125 ml
1 ½ cup	Sliced fruits (banana, mango, peach, berries, etc.)	375 ml

1. Mix the ingredients in a blender or food processor until smooth.
2. Add a bit of water if the mixture is too thick.
3. Pour the mixture into popsicle molds.
4. Freeze at least 3-5 hours or until set.

TIPS:

- Use homemade yogurt instead of coconut milk if tolerated. Freezing yogurt does not kill the probiotic bacteria. Coconut Yogurt (recipe, p. 214) also works great with this recipe.
- Sweeten to taste with honey or maple syrup, if tolerated.
- Avocado works also well and can add a nice creaminess to your popsicles, along with a nice boost of healthy fats and vitamin E.
- Don't have popsicle molds? Simple use muffin silicon molds! Pour in the popsicle mixture, place a popsicle stick in the middle, and freeze. If the popsicle stick won't hold because the mixture is too liquid, simply wait 30-60 minutes until it has started freezing to put it in.

notes:

Coconut Bark / contains coconut, nuts and dried fruits

This coconut bark recipe is so simple, yet it can give you the energy boost you need to accomplish whatever you have on your agenda for the day. Keep some on hand and break off a few pieces as needed. This coconut bark also makes an elegant treat that you can give away as a healthy gift for any special occasion. Be creative and use different combinations such as dried cranberries and walnuts, unsweetened dried coconut and lemon zest, or a mixture of chopped and roasted hazelnuts, macadamia nuts and pistachios.

Yields a 4 in x 6 in (10 cm x 15 cm) bark (depending on the thickness):		
1 cup	Coconut butter	250 ml
1 Tbsp	Coconut oil	15 ml
1 cup	Nuts, dried fruits and/or unsweetened dried coconut	250 ml

1. Put your glass jar of coconut butter in a large bowl. Fill it up with hot water and let rest for 5 minutes. This step will make your coconut butter easier to manipulate at room temperature.
2. Mix the coconut butter, coconut oil and any combination of tolerated nuts, unsweetened dried coconut, and/or dried fruits.
3. Spread the mixture on a lined baking sheet. Make it more or less thin, as preferred.
4. Put in the fridge until set.
5. Break the coconut bark into pieces.
6. Keep refrigerated in a hermetic container.
7. Take a few pieces when you need a quick sugar-free, caffeine-free energy boost.

TIPS:

- You can also pour the mixture into silicone muffin cups to obtain cookie-like coconut bark.
- **Chocolatey version.** Add 1-2 Tbsp (15-30 ml) of unsweetened cocoa powder and sweeten with a little bit of honey, maple syrup or coconut sugar, if tolerated.
- Coconut butter is sometimes also called coconut cream concentrate or coconut manna. It is not the same as coconut oil.

notes:

Tummy Gummies / contains fruit

Don't judge this recipe by its appearance! Although it might look like a kids' treat, it packs a nutritional punch. Gelatin is an excellent source of important amino acids, the building blocks of protein, that can contribute to gut healing. In addition, each fruity gelatin gummy is an excellent source of protein to maintain and repair your body. These tummy gummies are also fantastic to curb sugar cravings. Pop a few a day as a way to supplement your diet with gelatin, especially if you don't have Homemade Bone Broth (recipe, p. 176) on hand to support you on your healing journey.

Yields about 2 cups (500 ml):		
1 lb	Fruits, fresh or frozen (a single kind or a combination of strawberries, raspberries, blueberries, mango, peaches, pineapple, kiwi, etc.)	450 g
4-5 Tbsp	Gelatin powder (30-45 g)	60-75 ml
1/3 cup	Cold water	80 ml
A few drops	Vanilla extract (optional)	A few drops

1. In a small saucepan, heat the fruits (cut non-berry fruits into chunks) for about 20 minutes or until cooked and soft.
2. In the meantime, put the cold water in a wide bowl and sprinkle the gelatin over it. Let dissolve. This step is necessary to prevent the gelatin from forming lumps (which would happen if added directly to something hot without dissolving it first).
3. Once the fruits are soft, you can either mash them with a fork (for a chunkier consistency) or blend them in a food processor (for a smoother consistency). Wait until they cool to room temperature to prevent burning yourself.
4. Add the dissolved gelatin in the warm/hot cooked fruit mixture and whisk quickly to blend it in.
5. Transfer the fruit gelatin mixture to a glass dish lined with parchment paper. The size doesn't really matter but know that the larger the dish, the thinner your gelatin squares will be (and vice versa).
6. Let sit in the fridge for at least 2 hours until set.
7. Cut into 12 squares (or any shape you want).
8. Store in the fridge in an air-tight container and pop a few of your tummy gummies a day. 😊

TIPS:

- Strawberries, mangoes or blueberries work well for this recipe but you can experiment with a variety of different fruit combinations.
- Adjust the amount of gelatin until you find the consistency you prefer. The lower range will make your gummies softer and the upper range will make them more solid.
- Tummy gummies can keep in the fridge for at least 4-5 days. Enjoy as a treat or anytime snack.
- If you tolerate small amounts of sugar, you can try adding 1-2 Tbsp (15-30 ml) of honey, maple syrup or coconut sugar to the fruits in the first step when cooking them.
- Add ¼ cup (60 ml) of coconut milk to make the texture creamier and add more healthy fats to your diet. You might need to add an extra tablespoon (15 ml) of gelatin to maintain the same consistency since you're adding more liquid.
- Try to find high-quality gelatin (Great Lakes Gelatin Company is a good example).
- Pour the gelatin mixture into fun molds (step 5) to make your tummy gummies even cuter.

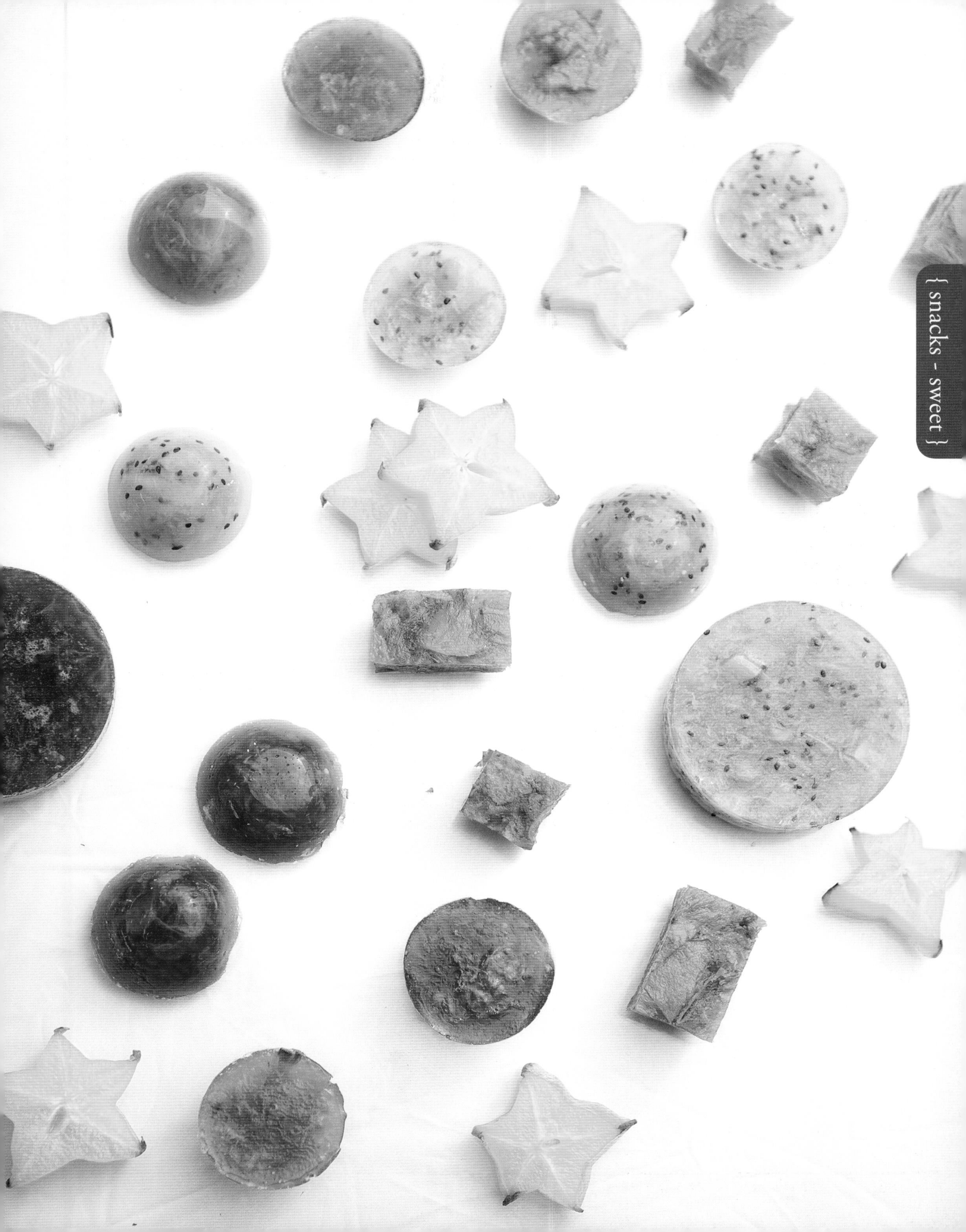

Banana Muffins / contains eggs, banana and coconut

As you know, most muffins you find in coffee shops or at the grocery store are far from being healthy foods. They're usually loaded with sugar, inflammatory vegetable oils, and irritating grains. Especially the healthy-looking low-fat bran muffins! The best way to enjoy muffins without damaging your health is, of course, to make your own! These banana muffins are much better for you. Not only are they free of the ingredients that can worsen your digestive problems, they are sugar-free and made of REAL food. Enjoy these muffins anytime as a snack or treat. You can even bake them as cupcakes and frost them with Coconut Whipped Cream (recipe, p. 192) once cooled down. If you don't tolerate eggs, try the egg-free version, called Muffin Libre (recipe, p. 90).

Yields 12 large muffins:		
1 ½ cup	Banana, mashed (about 3 medium)	375 ml
4	Eggs	4
1 cup	Melted coconut oil, ghee, butter or tallow	250 ml
1 tsp	Vanilla	5 ml
½ cup	Coconut flour	125 ml
1 tsp	Baking powder (optional)	5 ml
Dash	Unrefined salt	Dash
½ cup	Nuts, dried fruits or dark chocolate (optional)	125 ml

1. In a bowl, mix the wet ingredients: banana, eggs, melted fat and vanilla.
2. In another bowl, mix the dry ingredients: coconut flour, baking powder and seasonings.
3. Incorporate the liquid ingredients into the dry ingredients.
4. Pour the batter into a greased muffin tin or individual silicone muffin cups.
5. Bake in the oven at 350°F (180°C) for about 20-25 minutes or until a toothpick comes out clean.
6. Let cool and enjoy any time of the day. Spread with butter, ghee or coconut butter for extra healthy fats.

TIPS:

- **Banana chocolate muffins.** Add 1-2 Tbsp (15-30 ml) unsweetened cocoa powder and a bit of vanilla for a chocolate version.
- Make a double batch and freeze the extras. Thaw as needed.
- It is normal for the fat to sometimes separate from the muffins and boil around the batter while cooking. As the muffins cool down, the oil will be reincorporated into the muffins.
- **Banana-free version.** If you don't tolerate (or don't like) bananas, you can replace them with mashed/puréed avocado, plantains, butternut squash, or carrots.

Muffin Libre

/ contains bananas, coconut and flaxseeds; egg-free, nut-free, dairy-free and sugar-free

These muffins are called *libre*, which is Spanish for "free," because they are indeed free of the most common allergens such as eggs, nuts and dairy. They should also leave you *libre* of digestive problems after eating them! Flax seeds are used in place of eggs as a binder for this recipe. The high fiber content of flax seeds can be problematic if you're just starting out on the elimination diet, but your tolerance should improve once you get rid of the inflammation in your gut and allow it to heal with a REAL-food-based diet.

Yields 6 small muffins:		
2 Tbsp	Flax seeds, ground	30 ml
6 Tbsp	Water	90 ml
1 cup	Banana purée (about 2 medium bananas)	250 ml
½ cup	Dried shredded coconut, unsweetened	125ml
2 Tbsp	Coconut flour	30 ml
¼ cup	Coconut oil or ghee	60 ml
Optional	Vanilla extract, cinnamon, dried fruits or dark chocolate chunks	To taste

1. Start by letting the ground flaxseeds soak in the water for about 10 minutes.
2. Meanwhile, mix all the other ingredients.
3. Add the soaked flaxseeds (and the water they soaked in) to the batter and mix well.
4. Pour the batter into a greased muffin tin or individual silicone muffin cups.
5. Bake in the oven at 350°F (180°C) for about 20-25 minutes or until a toothpick comes out clean.
6. Let cool and enjoy.

TIPS:

- Double the recipe and freeze your extra muffins so you have a quick snack or treat on hand whenever needed.
- **Chocolate version.** Add 1-2 Tbsp (15-30 ml) unsweetened cocoa powder and a bit of vanilla.
- Always keep your ground flaxseeds in the freezer to prevent them from going rancid.

notes:

Main Meals: Chicken

Golden Chicken / appropriate for the elimination phase

If you make regular batches of digestive-health-aiding bone broth (as you learned to do in *DHwRF*), you probably also have a lot of chicken sitting in your fridge, waiting to be eaten. Although chicken's high protein content can help you stay full for a few hours, you can enhance its satiating power by combining it with plenty of fat. If you don't always like to slather your chicken in extra fat, try this recipe to learn how to incorporate more fat in your chicken to make it moister and more satisfying.

For each serving:		
4-8 oz	Cooked chicken	120-240 g
1-3 Tbsp	Ghee, coconut oil or duck fat	15-45 ml
To taste	Unrefined salt	To taste
To taste	Seasonings (thyme, rosemary, basil, oregano, garlic-infused oil, pesto, etc.)	To taste

1. Heat a skillet on medium-high with your preferred fat.
2. Meanwhile, shred your cooked chicken with your fingers or a fork.
3. Once the fat is melted and the skillet is hot, add the chicken and season to taste.
4. Stir often to make sure the chicken doesn't burn or stick to the skillet. Add more fat if needed. Stir-fry the chicken about 5-10 minutes until it's slightly golden.
5. Enjoy!

TIPS:

- Combine with vegetables you tolerate to create a simple and complete breakfast, lunch, snack or dinner!
- Once you tolerate butter, you can also try using this fat to prepare your golden chicken. Be careful with the temperature. Adjust it to prevent it from burning.
- Make your own ghee with good-quality butter, whether you want to follow the stovetop method explained on p. 246 of *DHwRF* or the easy slow-cook method on p. 160 of this cookbook.

notes:

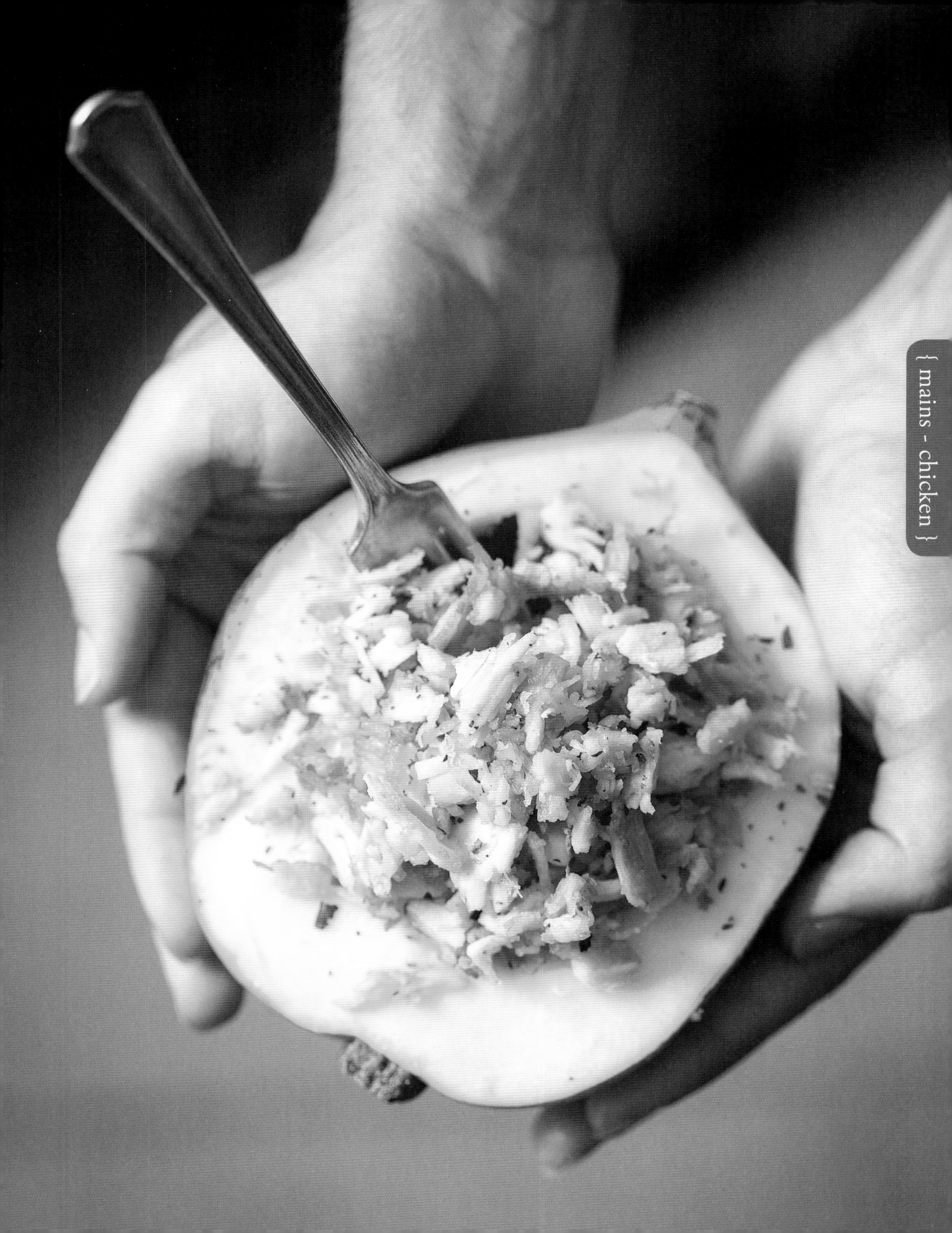

Lemon and Thyme Roasted Chicken

/ appropriate for the elimination phase

Most REAL foods don't naturally have the same satisfying crunch you get from processed foods like chips or crackers—but you can satisfy this craving with chicken skin. Although most people are afraid of eating chicken skin because of its high fat content, you now know that consuming more fat is necessary for you and that animal fat is not dangerous for your health. You can have your chicken and eat the skin, too!

Yields 2-4 servings:		
4	Chicken quarters (2 thighs + 2 breasts) with the skin	4
1	Lemon, sliced	1
1 Tbsp	Olive oil	15 ml
1 Tbsp	Thyme, dried	15 ml
To taste	Unrefined salt	To taste

1. Place the chicken quarters on a Pyrex tray.
2. Carefully lift the skin of the chicken breast and thighs and insert the lemon slices.
3. Drizzle the olive oil over the chicken quarters and sprinkle with salt and thyme.
4. Bake in the oven, under the grill, for 20-30 minutes or until thoroughly cooked and the skin is crispy. If your chicken is cooked (juices are clear and internal temperature reaches 165°F/74°C) but the skin is still not crispy, broil the chicken for 2-3 minutes until the skin is crispy (watch it closely so you don't end up with burnt chicken skin!).

TIPS:

- You can use garlic or use Garlic-Infused Oil (see recipe, p. 284 in *DHwRF* or the Garlicky Ghee recipe on p. 162 of this cookbook) instead of olive oil if you like.
- You can use this recipe with only chicken legs or chicken thighs if you prefer. You can also vary the seasonings by inserting, for example, garlic cloves or other combinations of herbs under the chicken skin.
- If you roasted your chicken plain without lemon and thyme, serve it with Chimichurri (recipe, p. 154), Herbed Ghee (recipe, p. 158), Guacamole (recipe, p. 166), Creamy Salad Dressing (recipe, p. 98) or Coconut-Asian Sauce (recipe, p. 168) to boost the flavor.
- Use the carcass of your roasted chicken to make Homemade Bone Broth (recipe, p. 176 of this cookbook or p. 244 of *DHwRF*).

Surprise Chicken Salad / contains bacon and egg yolks

What's the surprise in this salad? Bacon! The magic word that'll make anyone want to eat this salad. The elegant (and delicious) bacon nest takes this salad to a whole new level.

Yields 2 servings:			
Bacon nest	½-1 lb	Bacon slices	250-450 g
Creamy salad dressing (yields ½ cup or 125 ml)	½ Cup 1 1 Tbsp To taste To taste	Avocado oil Egg yolk Apple cider vinegar Unrefined salt Seasonings (chives, dill, garlic, etc.)	125 ml 1 15 ml To taste To taste
Salad	2-4 cups A few slices 4-12 oz To taste	Leafy greens (lettuce, spinach, etc.) Cucumber, radishes, etc. (as tolerated) Cooked chicken (sliced, cubed or shredded) Seasonings (salt, chives, cilantro, etc.)	0.5-1l A few slices 120-360 g To taste

Bacon Nests

1. Preheat the oven to 400°F (200°C).
2. Line the inside of two small baking dishes with aluminum foil. Choose baking dishes about the size of a normal salad bowl (make sure it's ovenproof).
3. Line bacon slices inside your small baking dishes, weaving them if desired.
4. Place the baking dishes on a baking sheet to prevent bacon fat from dripping in your oven.
5. Bake in the oven for 10-15 minutes or until crisp and golden.
6. Cool and carefully remove the bacon nests from the baking dishes.
7. You can collect the bacon fat and use it for cooking (or instead of the avocado oil to prepare the creamy salad dressing).

Creamy Salad Dressing

1. Put the egg yolk, apple cider vinegar and seasonings in a blender and mix.
2. With the blender on, pour the oil into the blender very slowly. The oil should emulsify (thicken) with the egg yolk as you pour the oil. Your creamy salad dressing can keep in a glass bottle in the fridge for about 5 to 7 days.

Salad

1. In a large bowl, combine the ingredients for the salad.
2. Add just enough of the creamy salad dressing to coat all the ingredients of your salad (without making it soggy).
3. Scoop the salad into the individual bacon nests and serve.

TIPS:

- Choose bacon made from pastured pork if you can. If you're sensitive to nitrates, try to find uncured or nitrate-free bacon instead. If you don't tolerate bacon, you can replace it with prosciutto (one of the only deli meats that is always free of gluten and other processed ingredients!).
- This creamy Ranch-like salad dressing is perfect as a dip for your kebabs and vegetables or as a sauce for your meat. Salad dressings don't have to be used for salad only. It's time to think (and eat) outside the box!
- If you don't tolerate garlic, use garlic-infused oil to prepare your homemade creamy salad dressing and give it a pleasant garlicky, FODMAP-free taste.
- Instead of chicken, you can also use beef and/or hard-boiled eggs as your protein for this recipe.

Main Meals: Red Meat

Grass-Fed Steak / appropriate for the elimination phase

Grass-fed beef is not only more nutritious than grain-fed beef, but it's also more flavorful. The most common mistake people make when trying grass-fed steak for the first time is overcooking it. Because of its different texture, grass-fed beef requires a shorter cooking time (by about 30 percent) and will be melt-in-your-mouth tender when cooked between medium-rare and rare. Good-quality steak requires very little seasoning because all the flavor you need is in the meat itself, but you can also serve your grass-fed steak with Chimichurri (recipe, p. 154), Caramelized Garlic (recipe, p. 156) Guacamole (recipe, p. 166) or Herbed Butter (recipe, p. 158) for some variety.

Yields 1-2 servings:		
¼-1 lb	Grass-fed steak	125-450 g
To taste	Seasonings (salt, pepper, etc.)	To taste
Optional	Chimichurri (recipe, p. 154)	Optional
Optional	Caramelized garlic (recipe, p. 156; contains FODMAPs)	Optional

1. Temper your steak by letting it sit at room temperature for about 30 minutes.
2. When ready to cook your steak, make sure your grill or pan is hot. Add bacon fat, coconut oil or ghee to prevent your steak from sticking to the grills or pan. Sear the steak by cooking it at high temperature for about a minute on each side, seasoning to taste on each side.
3. Once seared, lower the temperature to medium and cook for an extra 3-7 minutes on each side (depending on the thickness and desired doneness). Resist the temptation to poke the steak!
4. Your steak should be ready when it feels slightly firm to the touch. Remove from the heat and let rest on a plate for 5 minutes to allow its natural juices to redistribute. Don't cut it yet or you'll lose the precious juices!
5. Serve with the chimichurri sauce (safe for the elimination diet) and caramelized garlic (caution: contains FODMAPs) if desired.

TIPS:

- Experiment with different cuts of grass-fed steak like T-bone, New York strip, rib eye, sirloin or filet mignon to find your favorites. You can also marinate your meat in vinegar (balsamic or red wine, for example) or coconut aminos and a mixture of your favorite seasonings for 1-2 hours before cooking.
- Mashed cauliflower puréed with butter and grilled vegetables make a delicious and nutritious side dish for your grass-fed steak.

Divine Meatballs / contains FODMAPs (avocado) and bacon

Making your own meatballs is so easy. And you get to pick exactly the seasonings (and even stuffing) of your choice. It's also a lot safer, since commercially prepared meatballs tend to contain breadcrumbs or other wheat- and soy-derived ingredients. These meatballs contain only safe ingredients—and the divinely creamy texture of the avocado and savory crunchiness of the bacon hiding inside will pleasantly surprise your taste buds while keeping your tummy happy.

Yields 2-4 servings:		
1 lb	Ground beef	450 g
To taste	Seasonings (salt, pepper, chives, spices, herbs, etc.)	To taste
1	Avocado	1
4-6 slices	Bacon, cooked and chopped	4-6 slices

1. In a bowl, season the ground beef to taste. Break it with your hands or a wooden spoon and mix well.
2. In another small bowl, mash the avocado. Reserve.
3. To prepare your divine meatballs, take about 2-3 Tbsp (30-45 ml) of ground beef mixture and from a little ball. With your thumb, press on the center of the meatballs to form a little pocket. Stuff a little bit of mashed avocado and chopped bacon in the center and close the opening by shaping some of the ground meat mixture around it. Add more ground beef if needed.
4. Repeat step 2 until you've used up all of your ingredients. If you have extra mashed avocado, use it to make guacamole (recipe, p. 166).
5. You can bake your divine meatballs in the oven at 350°F (180°C) for about 20-25 minutes (depending on the size of your meatballs) or until golden and cooked throughout (best option if you're busy with something else and want a worry-free cooking method). Alternatively, you can cook your meatballs in a skillet for more flavors. Start by melting some ghee, butter, lard, bacon grease or coconut oil. Once the skillet is hot, add a single layer of meatballs. Cook under medium heat, turning every few minutes until golden on all sides. Repeat if you still have uncooked meatballs left.
6. Bon appétit!

TIPS:

- You can vary the meat with whatever type you like, such as ground bison, ground lamb, ground turkey or ground chicken. Vary the seasonings and find new stuffing for your meatballs to create endless possibilities.
- Other ingredients that can be used to stuff your meatballs, as tolerated, are puréed sweet potato, puréed carrot, prosciutto, olives, cold Herbed Butter (recipe, p. 158) or cheese.
- You can also experiment with different seasonings for your meat, such as chopped onions, olives, mushrooms, sun-dried tomatoes (a nightshade), Pesto (recipe, p. 136) or Chimichurri (recipe, p. 154).
- **Asian-inspired meatballs.** Make an Asian version of these meatballs by adding grated ginger, finely chopped green onions, grated carrots and a couple tablespoons of coconut aminos to the ground meat. Serve these meatballs with the Coconut-Asian Sauce (recipe, p. 168).
- You can prepare your meatballs in advance (then store them in the fridge) and cook them a few minutes before you're ready to eat to save time.

Mediterranean Burgers / customizable for the elimination diet

These Mediterranean burgers are simple yet delicious. This is the beauty of cooking with REAL food! Even if you don't have a lot of experience in the kitchen, you'll find that simply assembling quality ingredients is all you need to create delicious meals. As simple as that. If you're still on the elimination phase of the *DHwRF* protocol, use lettuce leaves as a bun, omit the olives and balsamic vinegar from the burger mixture, and use only toppings you tolerate.

Yields 2-4 servings:			
Burger	1 lb To taste ¼ cup ¼ cup Splash	Ground meat Seasonings (salt, pepper, chives, basil, oregano, thyme, etc.) Spinach, finely chopped Kalamata olives, pitted and chopped (optional) Balsamic vinegar	450 g To taste 60 ml 60 ml Splash
Grain-free "buns"	0 2-4 4-8 2-4	None (this burger is so good, you can eat it on its own!) Grilled Portobello mushrooms caps Cauli-buns (recipe, p. 56) Lettuce leaves	
Extra toppings (optional)	2-4 ½-1 cup A few slices ¼-½ cup ¼-½ cup	Fried eggs Guacamole (recipe, p. 166) Bacon, cooked Tapenade (pitted kalamata olives reduced to a chunky purée) Caramelized onions (recipe, p. 152)	2-4 125-250 ml A few slices 60-125 ml 60-125 ml

1. Prepare your burger mixture by mixing all the ingredients in a bowl. Form 2-3 large or 4-6 small patties. Cook in a skillet under medium heat, about 5-10 minutes per side (depending on the size and thickness).
2. Meanwhile, prepare your grain-free buns if you decided to use them. For the Portobello mushroom caps, grill them on a lined baking sheet at 400°F (200°C) for about 10-15 minutes or until soft. If you want to use the cauli-buns, follow the recipe on p. 56 and shape the dough into 4-6-in (10-12 cm) -wide circles to form your buns. If you're using lettuce leaves, simply wash a few and pat them dry.
3. Prepare the desired toppings.
4. Assemble your burgers with your chosen ingredients.
5. Enjoy with a salad or with homemade oven-baked vegetable fries made with either carrots, turnips, jicama, sweet potatoes or butternut squash for a complete meal (see *DHwRF* p. 272).

TIPS:

- Vary the meat with whatever type you like, such as ground bison, ground lamb, ground turkey or ground chicken.
- Double the recipe to make extra burgers for breakfast or lunch the next day.
- If you tolerate nightshades, add finely chopped sun-dried tomatoes to the meat mixture and use grilled eggplant slices as a bun.

Anticuchos / contains vinegar, cumin and garlic

Anticuchos are a traditional Peruvian recipe. Although they can be made with any cut of beef, they are traditionally prepared with beef hearts. If you've never had heart before, this is the perfect recipe to try it. Beef heart is technically an organ, but unlike liver, it has the familiar texture of muscle meat, with the extra bonus of being super tender and providing the anti-aging, heart-healthy antioxidant coenzyme Q10 (coQ10).

Yields 6-8 servings:			
Protein	1	Beef heart (about 2 lb or 1 kg)	1
Marinade	½ cup 2 2 Tbsp 2 Tbsp To taste	Red wine vinegar (or balsamic vinegar) Garlic cloves, minced Olive oil Cumin Salt and pepper	125 ml 2 30 ml 30 ml To taste
Other		Skewers (wood or metal)	

1. Cut the beef heart into cubes or strips, trimming the outer layer of fat and the inner membrane and stringy structures; this is easier when your beef heart is still semi-frozen. You can also ask your butcher to do this for you. Place in a bowl.
2. Combine all the marinade ingredients and whisk until homogenous (use a blender to make it easier).
3. Pour the marinade over the pieces of beef heart and let marinade for at least 4 hours or ideally overnight.
4. Thread 3-5 pieces on each skewer.
5. Grill your anticuchos on the barbecue (or in the oven at 375°F/190°C or the stove under medium-high heat) for a few minutes on each side depending on the thickness of your cubes (between 2-5 minutes on each side). Simply cook your beef heart to your preferred doneness for other cuts of meat.

TIPS:

- You can also use chili peppers if you want to make it spicier—just remember that these spices are nightshades.
- Serve with Guacamole (recipe, p. 166) or Chimichurri (recipe, p. 154) if desired.
- Slice your beef heart more thinly before marinating it and use it to make the Clean Jerky recipe on p. 72.

notes:

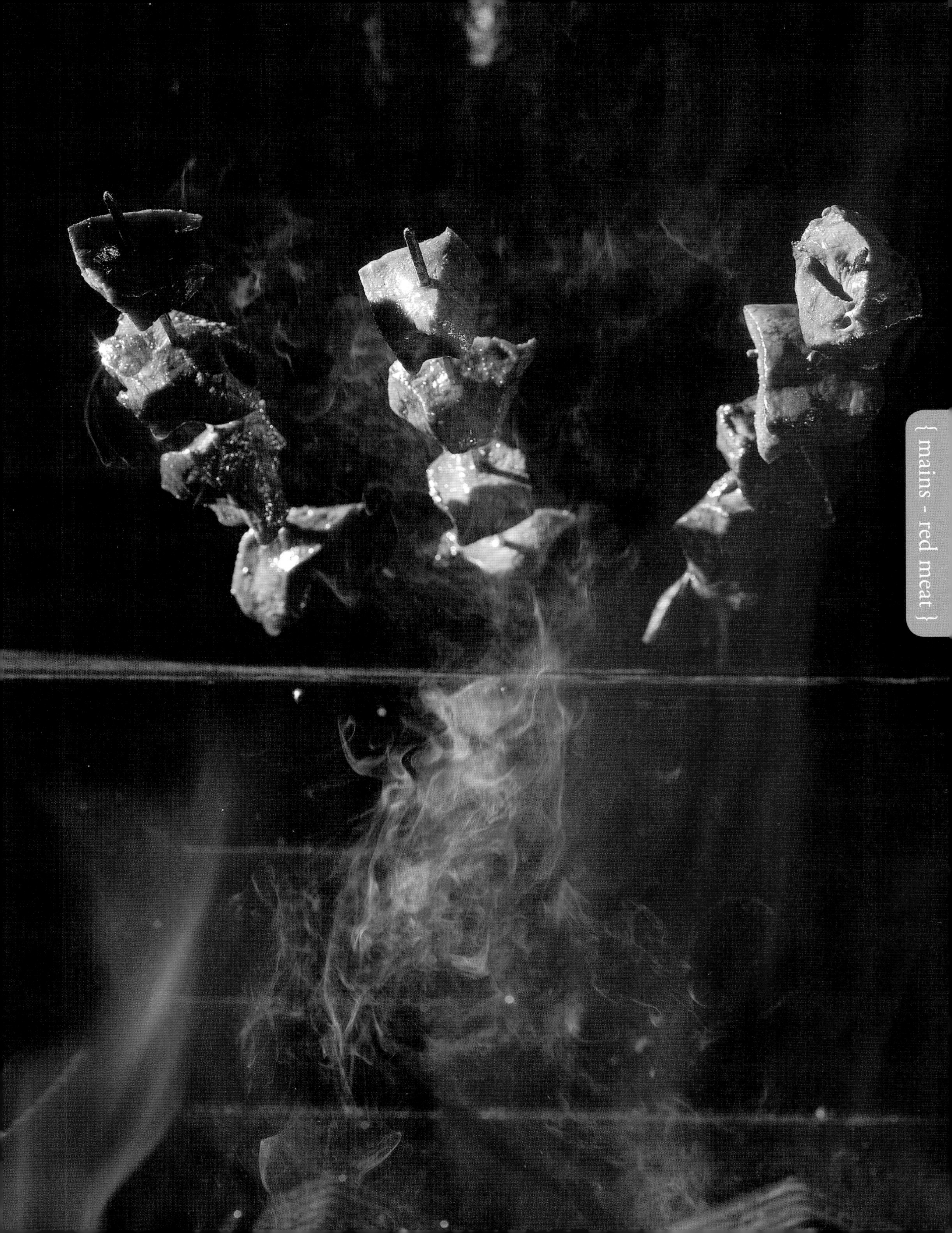

Grass-Fed Steak Tartare / contains egg yolks

Steak tartare is a classic French dish that consists of raw beef served with a variety of toppings. It's a real delicacy, especially if made of the best-quality REAL food you can find. Only use beef that comes from a trustworthy source, since you're going to be eating it raw—no grocery-store meat for this recipe, please! The same goes for the raw egg yolks.

Yields 2-4 servings:			
Meat	1 lb To taste Optional	Fresh top sirloin or tenderloin grass-fed steak Seasonings (salt and black pepper) Dijon mustard, extra-virgin olive oil and/or lemon juice	450 g To taste Optional
Sides	2-4 To taste To taste To taste	Egg yolks Green onions or chives, chopped (if sensitive to FODMAPs, avoid the white part of green onions) Parsley, chopped Fermented Pickles (see recipe, p. 216)	

1. Trim your meat of any visible fat and discard.
2. Chop your steak into thin strips with a large chef's knife.
3. Turn your cutting board 90 degrees and chop your thin strips again to obtain small (as small as you can) squares of steak.
4. Repeat a few more times, turning your cutting board by 90 degrees each time, until your steak resembles ground meat (but with a slightly coarser texture).
5. Transfer your chopped steak to a bowl and season to taste with salt and black pepper. Either leave your steak like that or add more seasonings, like 1 Tbsp (15 ml) of Dijon mustard, olive oil and/or lemon juice. Mix well.
6. Shape individual servings of steak tartare with your hands (or a small container) and place each of them at the center of a plate.
7. Decorate the plate with small amounts of chopped green onions, parsley and/or fermented pickles. Top each steak tartare with a raw egg yolk (directly on the steak tartare or within half of its cracked, washed egg shell).
8. Bon appétit!

TIPS:

- You can prepare all the side ingredients in advance except for the meat, which should be prepared right before serving for maximum freshness.
- Other good sides to serve with your tartare are capers, finely diced shallots and finely diced red onions (you can also incorporate some into the meat mixture).
- Avocado is not a traditional French topping for this recipe, but its creaminess complements this dish very well.
- Serve your steak tartare with a salad of raw or cooked vegetables and Creamy Salad Dressing (recipe, p. 98), or with oven-roasted vegetables fries like sweet potatoes, jicama, turnips, carrots or beets (see *DHwRF* p. 272).
- It's also possible to use ground meat for this recipe, but make sure that your meat was freshly ground and that you trust your source.
- Bison works also beautifully for this recipe.

Daylight Pasta / contains FODMAPs (beets); nightshade-free, grain-free and dairy-free

Many people who suffer from autoimmune conditions, joint pain or digestive problems unfortunately need to say goodbye to nightshades, a family of plants that includes tomatoes, bell peppers, hot peppers, paprika, eggplant, white potatoes and several other foods. If you miss your usual red pasta sauce, try this nightshade-free version. Don't expect it to taste exactly the same as regular tomato sauce, but if you keep your mind open to the wonderful flavors of REAL foods, I'm sure this recipe will soon become one of your new favorites, too.

	Yields 1-2 servings:		
Pasta	2-4 cups	Spaghetti squash or spiralized zucchini	0.5-1 l
	To taste	Seasonings (salt, pepper, basil, oregano, garlic, cooked onions, bacon, etc.)	To taste
	Yields 3-4 servings:		
Nightshade-free spaghetti sauce	3	Beets, peeled and chopped	3
	½-1 cup	Water or homemade bone broth	125-250 ml
	1-2 Tbsp	Coconut oil, ghee or lard	15-30 ml
	1	Onions, diced (optional)	1
	2	Carrots, diced	2
	½ cup	Mushrooms, sliced (optional)	125 ml
	1 lb	Ground beef	450 g
	To taste	Seasonings (salt, pepper, garlic, basil, oregano, thyme)	To taste

For the pasta:

Spaghetti squash	Spiralized vegetables
1. Cut it in half lengthwise and place it on a lined baking sheet.	1. Use a vegetable spiralizer to obtain zucchini pasta.
2. Bake the spaghetti squash for about 40-45 minutes or until you can easily insert a fork into it.	2. In a skillet, heat some coconut oil or ghee.
3. Let cool 10-15 minutes before shredding the flesh of the squash with a fork.	3. Sauté your zucchini pasta for 5-10 minutes until cooked.
4. Serve with your desired pasta sauce.	4. Serve with the desired pasta sauce.

For the sauce:

1. Place the chopped beets in a large pot, cover with water and bring to a boil. Cook for about 45-60 minutes or until easy to pierce with a fork.
2. Once cooked, drain the water and let cool.
3. In the meantime, heat your chosen fat in a large skillet and add the vegetables. Sauté until soft. When the vegetables are cooked, transfer to a larger pot.
4. Use the same skillet you used for the vegetables to cook the ground beef until no longer pink. Make sure you break it up as it cooks. Once cooked, transfer to the large pot with the cooked vegetables.
5. Now that your beets have cooled, transfer them to a blender or food processor. Add the water or homemade bone broth and process until smooth. You may need to stop and scrape the sides to ensure you obtain a perfectly smooth texture.
6. Transfer the puréed beets to the large pot with the cooked vegetables and meat. Reheat the sauce on medium.
7. Season to taste and serve over spaghetti squash or spiralized zucchini.

TIPS:

- This pasta sauce is chunky because of the diced vegetables. If you prefer a smoother sauce, simply put the cooked vegetables in the blender or food processor with the beets.
- A few slices of diced cooked bacon make a very nice addition to this recipe… But where would bacon not taste good?!

Fajitas de Lengua / appropriate for the elimination diet

This fajita recipe is delicious. Of course, you can make fajitas with a variety of meats, but lengua works particularly well. In fact, it's one of the favorite fajita fillings in Mexico. You can customize this fajita recipe using only the ingredients and condiments you tolerate. Or, simply serve the lengua on its own, along with stir-fried vegetables, for example. Lengua is that good, and it doesn't require much to go with it! And by the way, "lengua" means "tongue." Just call it "lengua" to prevent any mental block, and the surprisingly amazing taste and melt-in-your mouth texture of this cut of meat will do the trick.

Yields 6-8 servings:		
Basic	1 beef tongue Seasonings to taste (salt, herbs, etc.)	
Fajitas	Lettuce leaves or cauli-bread (recipe, p. 56) shaped as fajitas	* Cauliflower contains FODMAPs
	Vegetables (sliced bell peppers, tomatoes)	* Bell pepper and tomatoes are nightshades
	Guacamole (recipe, p. 166)	* Avocado contains FODMAPs
	Salsa (recipe, p. 134)	* Contains nightshade
	Creamy salad dressing (recipe, p. 98)	* Contains egg yolks
	Caramelized onions (recipe, p. 152)	* Contains FODMAPs

Beef Tongue

1. Thaw your beef tongue overnight if frozen.
2. Put the tongue in a slow cooker, cover with water and cook at low for about 8-10 hours. If you want, add bone broth, onions and other vegetables, but this is not necessary. If you don't have a slow cooker, you can simply boil your tongue in a large pot under low heat, ensuring that it's barely simmering.
3. After 8-10 hours, turn off the heat. Remove the tongue from your slow cooker, put on a glass baking dish and let cool for at least 15-20 minutes.
4. Once cooled enough so you can handle the beef tongue without burning yourself, peel off the outer layer of the tongue. Discard any bits that are hard.
5. Using a fork, shred the meat you extracted from the tongue. Season to taste.
6. Serve as is or use for the fajitas below.

Fajitas de Lengua

1. Before your meal, put all the desired ingredients on the table and let everyone build their own fajitas. Tip: Use a muffin pan (that you know hasn't been contaminated with gluten) to keep each fajita topping separate from each other without having to use a dozen bowls.
2. To prepare the fajitas, you can use either lettuce leaves or cauli-bread shaped as fajitas. Add the meat, desired vegetables and condiments.
3. Enjoy!

TIPS:

- If you're serving this recipe to the rest of your family or guests, just call it lengua or fajitas de lengua to make them more receptive to trying it. Tongue, heart or liver shouldn't be seen as disgusting, but unfortunately, many people have lost touch with where their food comes from. Eating every part of the animal is not only more respectful to the animal, but also provides a wider variety of tastes and nutrients.
- An average beef tongue yields around 1-1.5 lb (400-700 g) of meat.

Honey and Garlic Ribs / contains FODMAPs (honey), mustard and garlic

What's not to like about ribs? They melt in your mouth and usually come with a deliciously sweet sauce. Most pre-prepared or restaurant ribs unfortunately contain a considerable amount of sugar, in addition to other unnecessary additives like monosodium glutamate (MSG) or even gluten. To solve this problem, make your own ribs with clean ingredients and just a minimal amount of sugar.

Yields 4 servings:			
Meat	3 lb	Back ribs	1.5 kg
Marinade	6 Tbsp 6 2 Tbsp 4 Tbsp 2 Tbsp To taste	Dijon mustard Garlic cloves Mustard powder Honey Lemon juice Seasonings (salt and pepper)	90 ml 6 30 ml 60 ml 30 ml To taste

1. In a large pot of salted water, boil the back ribs for about 1 hour.
2. Drain and pat dry with paper towels. Place the ribs in a large baking dish.
3. Meanwhile, prepare the marinade by mixing all the ingredients.
4. Cover the ribs with the marinade and put in the fridge for at least 2 hours, but ideally 12 hours.
5. You can grill your ribs on the barbecue, turning them and basting them a few times. You can also bake them in the oven, with the marinade, at 400°F (200°C) for about 1 hour, turning them a few times.

TIPS:

- Although this recipe might look like it is high in sugar compared to other recipes in this cookbook, the sugar content actually corresponds to only 1 Tbsp (15 ml) of honey per person, or about 17 g of sugar per serving if you eat your complete share of the marinade. You'll get a lot less sugar if you eat only the part of the marinade that sticks to the ribs.
- If you're very sensitive to the FODMAPs in garlic, omit them and season with chives and peppercorns instead. You can also use maple syrup instead of honey if you don't tolerate fructose. Asafoetida powder (make sure it's gluten free) is another good seasoning that can give a FODMAP-free onion-like taste to your ribs.
- If you like the taste of mustard but don't like the sugar-loaded commercial ones, mix mustard powder with a small amount of water. Be warned that it will taste stronger than the commercial kind, but this is a great way to add a (clean) punch to your meals.

Two Shakes of a Lamb's Tail Stew / appropriate for the elimination diet

I had lamb for the first time when I had the opportunity to live in Australia for a year. Whenever I eat it now, it brings back wonderful memories of that incredible country. If you've never had lamb before, this is a good recipe to give it a try. If you feel restricted on your elimination diet and want to try something new, try lamb. Just be prepared: it's a completely different, but delicious, taste compared to any other meats.

Slow cooking is so simple, but also allows you to bring deep, complex and rich flavors to any of the REAL food ingredients you use. If you ignore the first 5-10 minutes of preparation, it's almost as though someone else prepared dinner for you! If you've never tried lamb, this is a great, easy first recipe that will get you hooked. This stew will give you easy leftovers for a few days. You can also start your stew before going to bed to have a nice breakfast or lunch waiting for you the next day. Slow cooking truly turns REAL food into fast food once you learn how to plan ahead!

Yields 4-8 servings:			
Basic	2 lb 2 Tbsp 2 Tbsp 2 Tbsp 2-3 cups To taste 4-6 cups 1-2	Stewing lamb (or any lamb part cubed) Olive oil Dried herbs (rosemary, parsley, etc.) Ghee, tallow or coconut oil Carrots, zucchini, green beans, etc. Seasonings (salt, asafoetida powder, etc.) Homemade Bone Broth (recipe, p. 176) or water Lamb or beef bones (optional)	1 kg 30 ml 30 ml 30 ml 500-750 ml To taste 1-1.5 L 1-2
Optional	Counts as part of the 2-3 cups of vegetables	Tolerated vegetables, cut into cubes (onions, leeks, garlic, celery, butternut squash, sweet potatoes, etc.)	Counts as part of the 500-750 ml of vegetables
	1 cup	Red wine (or ¼ cup or 60 ml of red wine vinegar)	250 ml

1. Although this step is optional, it can greatly enrich the flavor of your stew. You can first marinate your lamb overnight before cooking it in the slow cooker. Simply put your cubed lamb in a big bowl with the olive oil and dried herbs. You can add more herbs and/or use fresh herbs if you like. Cover and marinate in the fridge overnight.

2. This step is also optional. The next morning, you can quickly sear your meat and grill the exterior of your vegetables to add more depth to your stew. Heat the ghee (or other desired fat) in a skillet until hot. Add the lamb and stir a few times until slightly golden (it doesn't have to be fully cooked at this point). Transfer to your slow cooker. In the same pan, briefly grill your vegetables in the same way. Add more fat if needed. Once your vegetables are slightly grilled (they don't have to be fully cooked), transfer them to your slow cooker with the meat.

3. If you decide to skip the marinating (step 1) and grilling (step 2), start here. Put your meat, vegetables and seasonings in your slow cooker.

4. Add a bone or two (optional) and cover with bone broth or water.

5. Set at the lowest setting and cook the whole day (8-10 hours).

6. At the end of your day, turn off your slow cooker and let cool a few minutes while you take some time to relax before your meal. Don't worry—your stew will stay warm.

7. Serve and eat! Enjoy this stew with a side salad, over spaghetti squash, with a few slices of avocado or drizzled with extra healthy fats like olive oil or ghee.

TIPS:

- The quantities of ingredients used in this recipe will work well for a 6-quart (about 6 L) slow cooker. If your slow cooker is smaller, simply use about half the ingredients. If you don't have a slow cooker, you can also make this recipe on the stovetop or in the oven, using a large pot to simmer your stew. But I don't recommend leaving the stew on the stove if you're going out that day. Invest in a slow cooker—you won't regret it.

- If you can, find grass-fed lamb for more nutrition. Tip: Lamb from New Zealand or Iceland is usually grass fed, but you can probably also find some locally. Don't be afraid to ask around at your local butcher or at the farmer's market.

- Rosemary is a classic herb for lamb, but don't be afraid of experimenting with other seasonings. Give this stew a Greek twist by adding tomatoes and serving it on spaghetti squash or spiralized zucchini, or give it with a Moroccan punch with sweet potatoes, cumin, coriander, rosemary, ginger, cinnamon and a handful of dried apricots and serving it on cauli-rice (see *DHwRF*, p. 276).

- You can easily replace the stewing lamb with a leg of lamb. And for even more flavor, marinate it overnight and then roast it in the oven at 325°F (160°C) for about 25 minutes per pound (55 minutes per kilo) or until the internal temperature (not the bone) reaches 145-150°F (63-66°C). This will get you a medium-rare roasted leg of lamb, for peak tenderness and juiciness. Let rest a few minutes before carving and make a feast of this meal by accompanying it with mashed cauliflower and roasted vegetables (recipe, pp. 272 and 274 of *DHwRF*). This recipe works also wonderfully with stewing/cubed beef and bison.

Bison Multivitamin

/ appropriate for the elimination phase without the optional ingredients

If you're worried about the nutritional adequacy of your elimination diet because of the more limited food variety (you might be reassured by looking at the nutritional comparison in the *DHwRF* book on pp. 160-162), eating liver once or twice a week is even better than supplementing with a daily multivitamin. If you're afraid of eating liver, grinding it and mixing it with ground meat is a good way to get the unequalled nutritional value it provides (see sneaky burger recipe in the *DHwRF* book on p. 258). Or you can try the frozen liver supplement (recipe, p. 230). Of all the liver I've tried, bison liver has the mildest taste and the most pleasant texture. Even if you've had bad experiences with liver in the past, please give bison liver a chance! I really enjoy my bison liver cooked in bacon fat served with caramelized onions, a drizzle of balsamic vinegar and a few of slices of bacon as a treat.

Yields 1-2 servings:			
Basic	1-2 Tbsp ¼-1 lb To taste	Ghee, bacon fat or coconut oil Bison liver Seasonings (salt, pepper, etc.)	15-30 ml 125-450 g To taste
Optional	A few slices To taste Drizzle	Bacon, cooked Caramelized Onion Jam (recipe, p. 152) Balsamic vinegar	A few slices To taste Drizzle

1. Heat your fat of choice in a skillet on medium-high heat. If you choose to use bacon in this recipe, simply cook your bacon first. Once cooked, remove it from the skillet and use the bacon fat to cook the bison liver.
2. Cook the bison liver for 3-4 minutes on each side (when you see blood coming up on the top side). Season to taste on both sides (depending on the thickness of your liver). Make sure you don't overcook it!
3. Serve immediately with the desired toppings (balsamic vinegar, caramelized onion jam and/or bacon slices) accompanied with the vegetable of your choice (stir-fried broccoli, puréed turnips or homemade sweet potato fries).

TIPS:

- Many people are afraid of eating liver because they fear that toxins or waste products could accumulate in the liver of some animals. But you don't have anything to worry about. Yes, liver is a filtration organ but it doesn't *store* toxins. If you're still worried, choosing bison liver is another way of protecting yourself from exposure to harmful compounds, since almost all bison are 100 percent pastured and grass-fed, in addition to being free of antibiotics and hormones.
- You can try this recipe with any kind of liver (beef, lamb, etc.), but I find that bison liver has the mildest and most pleasant taste, smell and texture.
- **Bison Liver Pâté.** If you have leftovers, you can easily make a delicious bison liver pâté. Blend ½ lb (250 g) of cooked liver with ½ cup (125 ml) of cooked onions, a few slices of cooked bacon, ¼ cup (60 ml) of butter, ghee or bacon fat and seasonings to taste until you obtain a smooth purée. Serve your bison liver pâté over cucumber slices, Veggie Chips (see recipes p. 62) or Cauli-Bread (see p. 56). It's also great as a dip for vegetables.

Main Meals: Fish

Grain-Free Sushi / contains algae and FODMAPs (avocado and cauliflower)

Enjoying different cuisines at home is a cheap way to travel. Although it can be difficult to eat out when you have many food restrictions, many recipes can be adapted to be made at home without any grains, gluten or soy. This sushi recipe is made grain-free by substituting rice for grated cauliflower and soy sauce for coconut aminos. If you eat out at a Japanese restaurant, you can ask for sashimi and remember that anything containing soy sauce, tempura or imitation crab (surimi) contain gluten. Don't forget to bring your own coconut aminos or gluten-free tamari sauce.

Yields 1-2 servings:		
3-6	Nori sheets	3-4
1/3 - ½ cup	Cauliflower, grated	80-125 ml
½-1	Avocado, sliced	½-1
1	Carrot, julienne	1
3-6 oz	Smoked salmon or shrimp	90-180 g
2-4 Tbsp	Coconut aminos (or gluten-free tamari as tolerated)	30-60 ml

1. Dip the nori sheets in a bowl of warm water and place on parchment paper.
2. Spread the nori sheets with a thin layer of grated cauliflower (as a rice replacement) to cover most of the nori sheets except for ½ in (1 cm) at one end.
3. In the center of your nori sheets, line a few slices of avocado, julienne carrots and smoked salmon or shrimp.
4. Roll the sushi, starting with the cauliflower end of the nori sheet and going to the cauliflower-free end, as tightly as you can (use a bamboo mat if you like).
5. Cut each sushi roll into 6-8 pieces.
6. Enjoy your sushi dipped in coconut aminos (or gluten-free tamari sauce).

TIPS:

- If you don't like raw cauliflower, stir-fry the grated cauliflower in your favorite fat (coconut oil or ghee, for example) for a few minutes before using in this recipe. Just make sure you prepare it ahead so it has time to cool down before making your sushi.
- The fastest way to grate cauliflower is with your food processor or blender. Place florets in the processor or blender, cover with water and blend until you obtain small, rice-like chunks of cauliflower. Strain in a colander.
- You can use other vegetables, fruits and protein as tolerated. You can also use toppings like pickled ginger and wasabi, but make sure you read the ingredients carefully to avoid gluten or other problematic ingredients.
- With time, you may be able to tolerate white rice and use it instead of the cauliflower in this recipe.

Ceviche / appropriate for the elimination diet

This dish, pronounced *say-bee-chay*, originates from the coastal regions of Central and South America. I first had it in Lima (Peru) and loved it. As with other REAL food-based recipes, the quality of the ingredients is crucial—and make sure you use the freshest fish possible. The beauty of this recipe is that it doesn't involve any cooking. Even though the fish isn't cooked, it's not technically raw, either, since the acidity of the lime juice "cooks" it without any heat. Interestingly, the lime juice marinade used in ceviche is called leche de tigre or "tiger's milk"—but rest assured it's completely free of dairy (or tiger)!

Yields 2-4 servings:

Leche de tigre (marinade)	2/3 cup To taste 2 Tbsp Optional	Lime juice, fresh (about 8-12 limes) Seasonings (salt and black pepper) Cilantro, chopped Crushed garlic cloves, hot chili, red onion	175 ml To taste 30 ml Optional
Ceviche	1 lb A few sprigs To taste A few Optional	Fresh firm white fish fillets (fluke, tilapia, flounder, sole, etc.) Cilantro leaves Seasonings (salt and black pepper) Lettuce leaves Red onions, chopped	450 g A few sprigs To taste A few Optional

1. Combine all ingredients for the leche de tigre.
2. Cube the white fish and put it in a large non-reactive bowl (ideally glass or Pyrex, but not metal).
3. Add the leche de tigre and let the fish marinate in the acid of the lime juice for 15-60 minutes in the fridge or until the fish is white (no longer translucent).
4. To serve, prepare a small bed of lettuce in individual bowls.
5. Scoop the ceviche onto the lettuce leaves.
6. Drizzle with the leche de tigre.
7. Top with cilantro and chopped red onions (optional).

TIPS:

- Serve your ceviche with slices of avocado to add extra fat and creaminess to your meal.
- Mix equal parts of lime juice and lemon juice for the leche de tigre if you like.
- This meal is pretty low in fat. If you don't serve it with avocado, make sure you have something fatty to complete your meal (try the Coconut Fudge, p. 194; Coconut Bark, p. 84; Coconut MCT Balls, p. 78; MCT Bomb Smoothie, p. 80; Good-for-the-Tummy Tea, p. 206; Creamy Cream-Free Ice Cream, p. 184; or Banacado, p. 186).
- Ceviche is also often served with cooked sweet potatoes or fried plantains (see tips on how to make them on p. 32).

Grilled Salmon / appropriate for the elimination phase

Cold-water fatty fish like salmon contain a special kind of fat called omega-3 fatty acids (specifically, DHA and EPA). Omega-3 fats are known for their powerful anti-inflammatory qualities that can help calm the inflammation raging in your intestines and the rest of your body. Accompany this meal with your favorite combination of vegetables and traditional fats to make it complete.

Yields 3-4 servings:		
1 lb	Salmon fillets (fresh or frozen)	450 g
1-2 Tbsp	Olive oil	15-30 ml
To taste	Seasonings (salt, pepper, etc.)	To taste
3-4 Tbsp	Herbed Ghee (recipe, p. 158)	45-60 ml
1	Lemon	1

1. Place your salmon fillets in a baking sheet (lined with parchment paper to make cleaning easier).
2. Drizzle with olive oil and sprinkle with salt and pepper to taste.
3. Bake at 350°F (180°C) for 20-25 minutes depending on the thickness of the salmon and whether they were fresh or frozen. You'll know your salmon fillets are cooked when the flesh is no longer translucent and easily flaked with a fork.
4. In the meantime, prepare your herbed ghee. Dill is a good choice that goes particularly well with salmon.
5. Serve the salmon fillets with lemon wedges and a side of herbed ghee or butter. You can either spread the herbed ghee on the fish or use it as a dip.

TIPS:

- Whether you choose fresh or frozen salmon, make sure it's plain—or at least that the seasonings used are free of gluten and other problematic ingredients.
- Try to find wild-caught seafood instead of farmed. Not only is wild-caught fish more nutritious, it will also be free of soy, corn, wheat and other inflammatory and unnatural foods found in the feed of farmed fish.
- Salmon is also delicious served with a few slices of avocado or with Guacamole (recipe, p. 166).

notes:

Omega Boost Salad / appropriate for the elimination diet

Fish is known to be a great source of healthy omega-3 fats, but sardines actually rank higher than most other fish varieties. In addition, the fact that sardines are caught small and young means that they have lower levels of contaminants like mercury. Eat this omega boost salad two or three times a week to get all the omega-3 fats you need without having to supplement. In addition, most sardines are canned with their bones. But don't worry—they're so small and soft that they'll melt in your mouth, and big enough to add a nutritional punch. Bones are rich in many minerals, including calcium, that can help you keep your bones strong even on a dairy-free diet.

Yields 1 serving:		
1-2 cups	Green beans, steamed	250-500 ml
¼ cup	Grated carrots (raw or cooked)	60 ml
3-6 oz	Canned sardines, ideally with the bones, in water or olive oil	90-180 g
1-2 Tbsp	Extra-virgin olive oil	15-30 ml
1 Tbsp	Lemon juice, fresh	15 ml
To taste	Seasonings (salt, pepper, parsley, and other fresh herbs)	To taste

1. Open your canned sardines. Leave them whole or cut them into 2 or 3 pieces.
2. Put all the ingredients in a bowl.
3. Season to taste and serve!

TIPS:

- If you don't do well with green beans, you can substitute them with spinach (cooked or raw) or any other vegetable of your choice.
- Try to find sardines caught in the wild and packaged in a BPA-free can.
- You can also use canned salmon for a **quick salmon salad**. After opening the can, discard the skin and place the salmon with the bones in a bowl. Use a fork to mash the bones completely, then use the mashed salmon in the omega boost salad or with any combination of your favorite vegetables and seasonings. Add a few slices of avocado and a few spoonfuls of Guacamole (recipe, p. 166) or Creamy Salad Dressing (recipe, p. 98) for extra fats.

notes:

Main Meals:
Variable Protein

Speedy Recovery Soup / appropriate for the elimination diet

If you have a bad food reaction, whether it is part of the reintroduction protocol, from an involuntary cross-contamination, or simply going off track, this soup can help you recover more quickly by supplying all the nutrients you need to heal your damaged gut. Make sure you also rest enough and get at least eight or nine hours of sleep per night to speed up your recovery and feel healthy again.

Yields 1 serving:

2-4 Tbsp	Healthy fats (coconut oil, ghee, tallow, lard)	30-60 ml
2-3	Bones of your choice (or the carcass of a chicken)	2-3
2-4 cups	Tolerated vegetables (carrot, zucchini, squash, cauliflower, onions)	0.5-1 L
12-16 oz	Meat (chicken or beef cubes for example)	360-480 g
4-8 cups	Water	1-2 L
2-4 Tbsp	Vinegar (optional, i.e. coconut vinegar, apple cider vinegar, etc.)	30-60 ml
To taste	Seasonings of your choice (salt, pepper, basil, thyme, etc.)	To taste

1. Start by heating the healthy fats in a large pot under medium heat.
2. Add your choice of cut vegetables and sauté a few minutes to grill them on each side.
3. Remove the vegetables from the pan and do the same with the meat you want to use for your soup. Remember that you don't need to cook the meat at this point—just brown it quickly to add more depth to your soup. The meat will have plenty of time to cook while the soup is boiling.
4. Add the vegetables back to the pot or to your slow cooker. Add bones and fill with water. Season to taste. You can also transfer everything to a slow cooker if you prefer.
5. Cook on low for at least 2 hours, but ideally 6-8 hours, to make the soup easier to digest and extract more gut-healing nutrients from the bones.
6. When ready, carefully remove the bones and serve. If you want to make removing the bones easier next time, wrap them tightly in cheesecloth. All you'll have to do is remove the little bundle of bones instead of having to fish them out.
7. Store leftovers and reheat later for a quick gut-healing snack or meal.

TIPS:

- If you feel low on energy or have lots of cravings, try serving your soup with an additional spoonful of healthy fats (like ghee, coconut oil, or olive oil) or a couple of egg yolks.
- You can boost the recovery power of this soup by serving it with a few spoonful of sauerkraut or fermented foods. Just make sure the soup isn't too hot (not burning your mouth) when adding the fermented food to avoid killing their gut-friendly bacteria.
- Use bones from grass-fed, pastured animals if possible.
- Adding vinegar will help leech more body-balancing and rehydrating minerals from your bones.
- To speed up your recovery, make sure you sleep at least 8-9 hours a night, that you base your diet on nutrient-dense, anti-inflammatory foods, and that you manage your stress management (with meditation, relaxation, music, slow yoga, or other relaxing hobbies).
- If you have to be on a liquid diet because of a surgery or dentistry work, blend this soup and drink it to get all the important nutrition your body needs to heal.
- **Healing boost.** To boost the gut-healing potential of your soup, add (carefully washed) chicken or pig feet to make it extra gelatinous. Alternatively, you can sprinkle gelatin and L-glutamine powder into the soup for extra healing power. Great Lakes gelatin (greatlakesgelatin.com) makes good-quality gelatin from grass-fed, pastured animals. Mix 1-3 teaspoons (5-15 ml) of gelatin in 1 Tbsp (15 ml) of cold water until dissolved, then add it to your bowl of soup right before serving. The L-glutamine powder (500-1,000 mg) can be added directly to your hot soup.
- If you're having a food reaction, taking activated charcoal or an Epsom salt bath might also be beneficial.
- **Speedy Recover Stew.** You can also transform this soup into a speedy recovery stew. Use all the same ingredients, but with only half as much water. Throw all the ingredients in a slow cooker and cook on low for 6-10 hours overnight or during the day.

Grain-Free Pizza / contains FODMAPs (cauliflower) and eggs

This pizza recipe is a fun way to diversify your diet once you've gone through the elimination diet phase and have successfully reintroduced cauliflower and eggs. Choose different combinations of sauces, vegetables, proteins and toppings according to your own tolerance. You can even serve this grain-free pizza to your family and friends—it's so tasty that no one will miss the gluten-y crust!

Yields 2-4 servings:			
Dough	1 batch	Cauli-Bread dough (recipe, p. 156)	The cauliflower dough can be substituted with grilled eggplant slices or Portobello mushroom caps according to your personal tolerance.
Sauce	½-1 cup (125-250 ml)	Tomato sauce (recipe, p. 146)	Contains nightshades
		Nightshade-free red sauce (recipe, p. 112)	Contains FODMAPs (beets and onions)
		Chimichurri (recipe, p. 154)	Safe for most people
		Pesto	Make it yourself by combining ¼ cup (60 ml) of olive oil and 2 cups (500 ml) of basil or other fresh herbs to avoid the nuts and dairy found in commercial versions.
Vegetables	As tolerated	Onions, bell peppers, broccoli, kale, spinach, mushrooms,	Choose a combination of vegetables you tolerate.
Protein	At least 3 oz (90 g) per person	Cooked chicken, cooked ground beef, smoked salmon, cooked chorizo, cooked sausages, shrimp, etc.	Some chorizo and sausages may contain wheat, gluten or nightshades. Always read the ingredients carefully.
Toppings	A handful	Avocado, olives, fresh herbs (basil, dill, thyme, etc.), bacon, prosciutto, cherry tomatoes, artichoke heart, garlic, cheese, etc.	Choose a combination of toppings you tolerate.

1. Preheat the oven to 350°F (180°C).
2. Prepare the cauliflower dough as explained on p. 56. You can add a variety of seasonings to the cauliflower dough if desired (chopped olives, fresh or dried herbs, crushed garlic cloves, sun-dried tomatoes, etc.).
3. Spread the dough on a large, lined baking sheet to form either a circular or rectangular pizza crust. You can curl the borders a little bit if you want to mimic a regular pizza crust.
4. Bake the cauliflower crust for about 20-30 minutes (depending on the size and thickness) or until it turns golden brown.
5. Remove the cauliflower crust from the oven and increase the temperature to 400°F (200°C).
6. Prepare your pizza by layering the desired sauce, vegetables, protein and toppings.
7. Return to the oven and bake for an additional 10-15 minutes.

TIPS:

- If you have trouble digesting raw vegetables, steam or stir-fry them for a few minutes before adding them to your pizza.
- If you enjoy eggs, you can crack a few onto your pizza toppings right before putting it back in the oven for the last step.

Naked Wraps / contains raw vegetables, FODMAPs (avocado) or egg yolks

If you miss the convenience of sandwiches, this wrap recipe will help you forget bread for good. After all, isn't the best part of a sandwich the filling? This is especially true if you use your favorite combination of animal protein, vegetables, and seasonings. Without bread, these naked wraps filled with tasty ingredients are at least twice as nutrient dense as any regular sandwich, especially if you choose quality ingredients.

Yields 1-2 servings:				
Basic		2-6	Lettuce leaves, cabbage leaves, endives or Cauli-Bread (recipe, p. 56)	2-6
		1-2 Tbsp	Ghee, lard or coconut oil	15-30 ml
		To taste	Vegetables, as tolerated (onions, carrots, bell peppers, mushrooms, etc.)	To taste
		4-12 oz	Cooked slices of chicken, fish, pork or beef, canned tuna or smoked salmon	120-360 g
		To taste	Seasonings (salt, pepper, garlic, cumin, lime juice, etc.)	To taste
Optional	**Guacamole**	¼-½ cup	Guacamole (see recipe below)	60-125 ml
	Mayonnaise	¼-½ cup	Creamy Salad Dressing (recipe, p. 98 or p. 288 of *DHwRF*)	60-125 ml
	Quick Salsa	½ cup	Diced tomatoes (nightshade)	125 ml
		1 Tbsp	Diced onions (FODMAP)	15 ml
		1 tsp	Chili powder (nightshade)	5 ml
		To taste	Seasonings (salt, pepper, etc.)	To taste

1. Cut the vegetables of your choice into fine strips.
2. In a skillet, heat the 1-2 Tbsp of fat. When melted, cook the vegetable of your choices. You can also keep your vegetables raw if you prefer and if your digestive system is able to tolerate raw food.
3. Once cooked, add your choice of cooked protein (chicken, fish, pork or beef for example), season to taste and mix well.
4. Serve your wrap filling in lettuce, cabbage leaves, endives or cauli-bread.
5. Top with guacamole, mayonnaise or salsa as desired. Wrap tightly and enjoy.

TIPS:

- Ground meat, canned fish or hard-boiled eggs also work very well for this recipe.
- You can pack your naked wraps for lunch. Just store the filling and lettuce leaves separately and assemble when ready to eat.
- Nori sheets also work nicely as a wrap. Simply dip one in warm water to make it more flexible before filling and wrapping it.
- Another quick and easy way to prepare your lunch is to use deli meat to make your wrap (just make sure the deli meat is gluten free; prosciutto is usually a safe choice). Add mayonnaise, butter, guacamole, vegetables or other seasonings of your choice, wrap and enjoy!

Asian Noodle Bowl / contains kelp, coconut and nuts

Typical Asian noodle bowls are served over rice or rice noodles. Although rice doesn't contain gluten, people with various digestive problems may still experience issues with gluten-free grains. In addition, most sauces and seasonings used in these dishes contain soy, wheat or monosodium glutamate (MSG). This homemade Asian noodle bowl uses grain-free kelp noodles (made from algae) and is a great way to satisfy your cravings for something more exotic without the usual tummy troubles.

Yields 1-2 servings:		
1-2 cups	Kelp noodles	250-500 ml
1-3 Tbsp	Coconut oil, ghee or butter	15-45 ml
1-3 cups	Tolerated vegetables (onions, garlic, zucchini, carrots, broccoli, bok choy, kale, cabbage, bell peppers, mushrooms, etc.)	250-750 ml
4-12 oz	Cooked protein (chicken, pork, beef, fish, shrimp, etc.)	120-360 g
¼-1 cup	Coconut-Asian sauce (recipe, p. 168)	60-250 ml

1. Cut your chosen vegetables in julienne or small pieces. The smaller the pieces, the quicker your stir-fry will be ready!
2. In a wok or large skillet, heat the fat on medium-high. When melted, add the vegetables and stir-fry for 5-10 minutes, stirring often.
3. Meanwhile, prepare your kelp noodles following the directions on the package. Usually, all you need to do is rinse them in water and cut them to the desired length.
4. When the vegetables are cooked to your liking, add the kelp noodles and cooked protein. Mix well.
5. Add the prepared coconut-Asian sauce and serve.

TIPS:

- If you don't want to use coconut-Asian sauce, you can simply season your Asian stir-fry by adding grated ginger and coconut aminos.
- Coconut aminos is a soy- and gluten-free version of soy sauce made from the sap of coconut trees. It can be found in most health-food stores.
- Kelp noodles are an excellent source of iodine, an important mineral for optimal thyroid function that can be hard to get if you're no longer using iodized table salt.
- If you can't find kelp noodles, you can use spaghetti squash, spiralized zucchini, or cauli-rice (recipe, p. 276 of *DHwRF*).

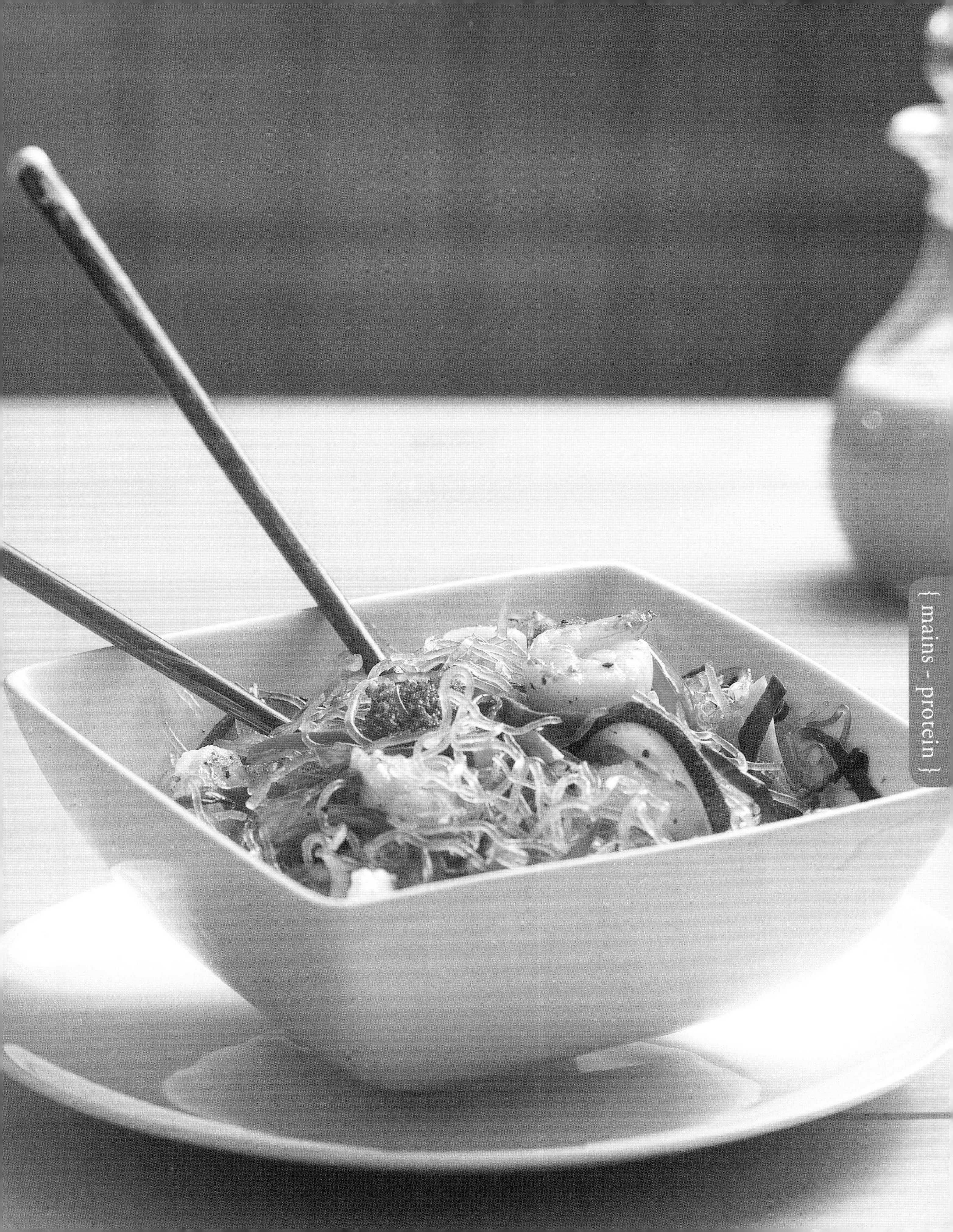

Aguacate Relleno / contains FODMAPs (avocado) and eggs

The quality of the ingredients is what makes this simple dish a success. I first had it when I was traveling in Peru and Ecuador. Ironically, this is where my digestive problems all started, but I still don't regret visiting these astonishingly colorful and culturally rich countries. I'm also very grateful that I can now enjoy avocado and eggs again without suffering. This recipe is a good way to incorporate more healthy fats into your diet.

For each serving:		
4-8 oz	Chicken, tuna, or shrimp, cooked	120-240 g
½-1 ½	Avocado, ripe	½-1 ½
1-3 Tbsp	Creamy Salad Dressing (recipe, p. 98)	15-45 ml
1-2 Tbsp	Lime juice	15-30 ml
To taste	Unrefined salt and pepper	To taste
To taste	Cilantro (optional)	To taste

1. If using chicken or tuna, cut it into cubes or shred it. Shrimps can be left whole but should be ready to eat (shelled and deveined). Put in a bowl.
2. Cut your avocado lengthwise (around the seed). Open the two halves, remove the seed and carefully peel them. Keep one or two peeled avocado halves intact for the presentation.
3. Cut the other avocado half into cubes and add to the bowl containing the cooked protein.
4. Add the homemade creamy salad dressing, lime juice and unrefined salt to taste. Gently mix until all ingredients are coated. Add more or less mayonnaise and lime juice until you get just the right consistency and taste.
5. Serve the protein mixture over your one or two avocado halves. Decorate with cilantro.
6. Enjoy!

TIPS:

- You can add diced red onion, garlic, finely chopped celery and radishes.
- This South American dish is traditionally served on a bed of lettuce with a few slices of hard-boiled eggs.
- You can also use eggs (fried, poached or hard-boiled) as your protein.
- This recipe also makes a perfect snack. Although it's better fresh, you can also make a larger batch and store it in the fridge, tightly wrapped with a plastic wrap to prevent oxidation of the avocado.
- The mayonnaise recipe on p. 288 of *DHwRF* works also perfectly well for this recipe instead of the Creamy Salad Dressing if you have it on hand.

Dreamy Creamy Pasta / contains FODMAPs (avocado)

Grain-based pasta, whether it contains gluten or not, is not really conducive to optimal digestive health—but the good news is that you can still enjoy pasta made from REAL, unprocessed, anti-inflammatory foods like the ones in this creamy pasta recipe. Spaghetti squash is a wonderful substitute for pasta, but I also really enjoy using spiralized zucchini (zucchini shaped into long pasta using a vegetable spiralizer like the Spirooli). In addition to getting your full serving of vegetables, this meal also provides you with healthy fats from avocado. Make this meal complete by adding a protein like chicken, fish, or eggs.

Pasta	Yields 1-2 servings:		
	2-4 cups To taste Optional	Spaghetti squash or spiralized zucchini Seasonings (salt, pepper, basil, oregano, garlic, cooked onions, bacon, etc.) Cooked chicken, fish, beef, hard-boiled eggs or cheese	0.5-1 l To taste Optional
Avocado Sauce	Yields about 1 cup (250 ml):		
	1 large 1-2 Tbsp 1-2 Tbsp To taste	Avocado (or 2 small) Olive oil, coconut oil or avocado oil Lemon or lime juice Unrefined salt and seasonings (cilantro)	1 large 15-30 ml 15-30 ml To taste

For the pasta:

Spaghetti squash	Spiralized vegetables
1. Cut in half lengthwise and place it on a lined baking sheet. Bake the spaghetti squash for about 40-45 minutes or until you can insert a fork easily. Then let cool 10-15 minutes before shredding the flesh of the squash with a fork. 2. While the squash is cooking, prepare the avocado sauce following the recipe below. 3. Combine the spaghetti squash with the avocado sauce, seasonings and optional protein and serve.	1. Use a vegetable spiralizer to obtain zucchini pasta. 2. In a skillet, heat a bit of coconut oil or ghee and sauté your zucchini pasta about 5-10 minutes until cooked. 3. Meanwhile, prepare the avocado sauce following the recipe below. 4. Combine the cooked zucchini pasta, avocado sauce, seasonings, and optional protein and serve.

For the sauce:

1. Peel the avocado and remove the seed.
2. Mix all the sauce ingredients in a blender.
3. Blend until smooth. If the dressing is too thick, add a bit more oil and blend until you reach the desired consistency. The avocado sauce can keep for about 5-6 days in the fridge (cover tightly to prevent browning).
4. Mix the avocado sauce with the pasta and serve topped with your desired seasonings and protein option.

TIPS:

• If you get a vegetable spiralizer, don't limit yourself to just zucchini pasta. Be creative with all kinds of vegetables as a base for this creamy pasta dish. Sweet potatoes, carrots, beets, turnips and butternut squash work very well for this recipe.

• If you don't have a vegetable spriralizer, you can use a mandoline (watch your fingers) or just cut the zucchini into spaghetti-shaped strings of zucchini by hand.

• Avocado is a great source of healthy and stable fats naturally packaged with a bonus of vitamin E and various antioxidants. Avocado does contain some FODMAPs and a lot of fiber that can be hard to tolerate for some people at first. Start with small amounts to assess your tolerance.

• Add a whole bunch of cilantro to give it a refreshing flavor.

• Instead of the avocado sauce recipe, mix equal amounts of avocado and Creamy Salad Dressing (recipe, p. 98) in a blender to obtain a creamy avocado sauce to use on your vegetables, drizzle on your meat or use as a dip for your shrimp, fish, or chicken. Both versions of the recipe can be used as a salad dressing, too.

Double GF Spaghetti / contains nightshades

This basic tomato sauce recipe is super easy to make and, unlike commercial varieties, it doesn't contain any processed ingredients. "Double GF" means it's free of grains and gluten. Making your own tomato sauce is a good way to avoid added sugar, as well as FODMAPs, if you're sensitive to them. You can add ground meat or meatballs to this sauce and serve it over zucchini noodles or spaghetti squash for a grain-free pasta meal.

Pasta	Yields 1-2 servings:		
	2-4 cups To taste	Spaghetti squash or spiralized zucchini Seasonings (salt, pepper, basil, oregano, garlic, cooked onions, bacon, etc.)	0.5-1 L To taste
Avocado Sauce	Yields 3 cups (750 ml):		
	3 cups 2 Tbsp To taste To taste 1-2 2-3	Fresh tomatoes, chopped Olive oil Unrefined salt Fresh or dried herbs (basil, oregano, thyme, etc.) Medium onion, chopped (optional) Garlic cloves, minced (optional)	750 ml 30 ml To taste To taste 1-2 2-3

For the pasta:

Spaghetti squash	Spiralized vegetables
1. Cut in half lengthwise and place it on a lined baking sheet. 2. Bake the spaghetti squash for about 40-45 minutes or until you can insert a fork easily. 3. Let cool 10-15 minutes before shredding the flesh of the squash with a fork. 4. Serve with your desired pasta sauce.	1. Use a vegetable spiralizer to obtain zucchini pasta. 2. In a skillet, heat a bit of coconut oil or ghee. 3. Sauté your zucchini pasta about 5-10 minutes until cooked. 4. Serve with your desired pasta sauce.

For the sauce:

1. Heat the olive oil on medium in a large saucepan.
2. If using garlic and onions, add them and cook until transparent.
3. Add the fresh tomatoes and bring to a boil. Cook until most of the liquid evaporates, or about 20-30 minutes.
4. Add the seasonings to taste (unrefined salt and fresh herbs).
5. The sauce is ready if you like it chunky. If you want a smoother sauce, use a hand blender or transfer it into a blender or food processor once it has cooled and process until you reach the desired consistency.
6. Serve over your grain-free pasta.

TIPS:

- Add 1-2 lb (450-900 g) of cooked ground meat to make this a complete meal.
- Use garlic-infused olive oil and a pinch of asafoetida powder (make sure it's free of gluten-containing fillers) to replace the garlic and onion if you're sensitive to FODMAPs.
- Add about 1 cup (250 ml) of diced carrots, sliced zucchini, sliced mushrooms, diced celery, or any other vegetables you tolerate for a nutrition boost.
- You can add ½ cup (125 ml) of red wine, 2 Tbsp (30 ml) of balsamic vinegar or 2-4 Tbsp (30-60 ml) of sun-dried tomatoes if desired.
- Freeze your tomato sauce and thaw as needed.

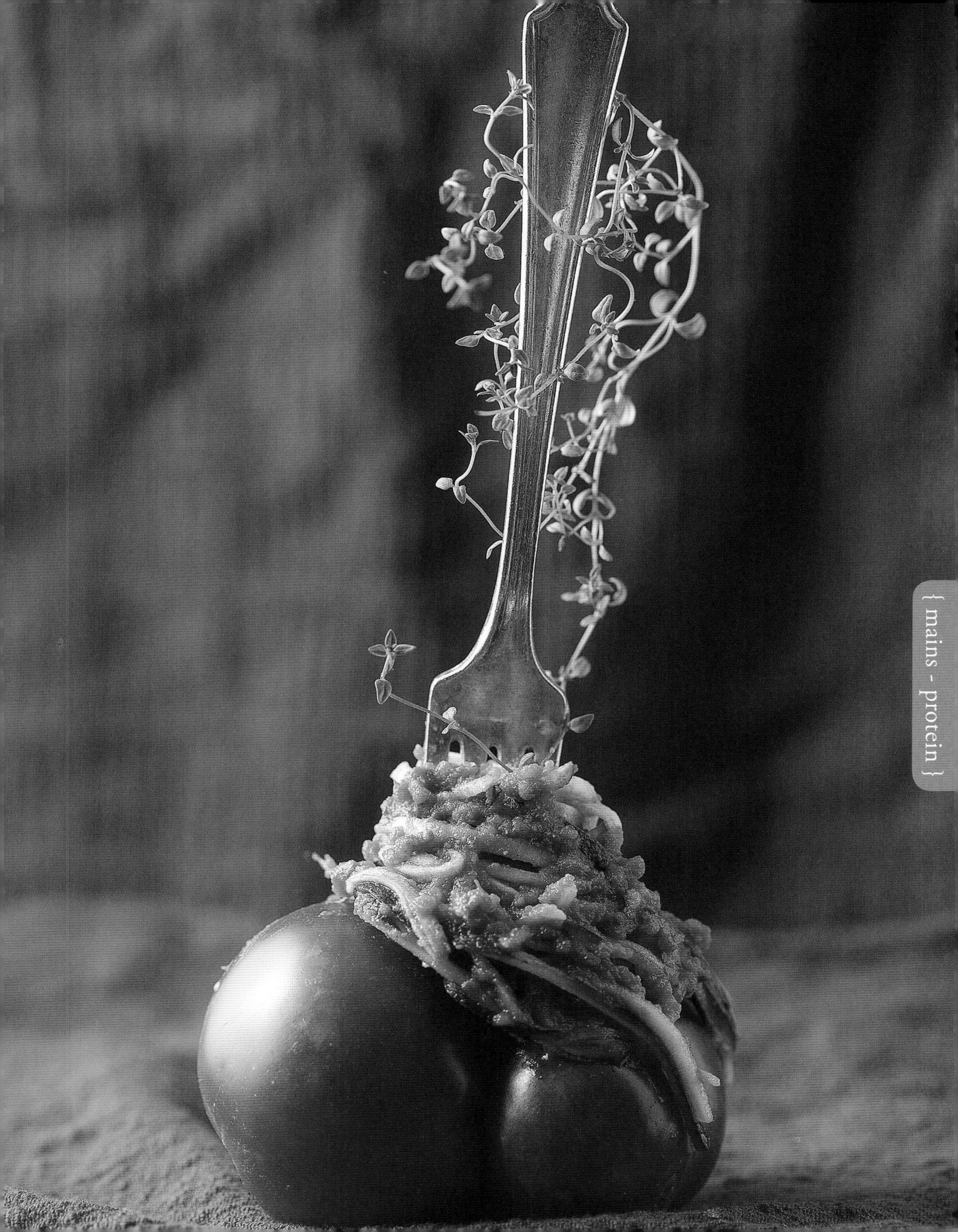

Lasachini / contains FODMAPs (beets); nightshade-free, grain-free and dairy-free

The *DHwRF* protocol can be very helpful in improving your digestion, but it can also be difficult to remove staple foods like grains and dairy from your diet. If you want to create meals that resemble former favorites, this lasachini recipe will let you feel like eating "normal" food like everyone else, with the comfort of knowing that this REAL food is actually good for you and your loved ones.

Yields 3-4 servings:		
3 large	Zucchini (amount depends on the size and thickness of the slices)	6 small
2-3 Tbsp	Ghee, coconut oil or lard	30-45 ml
1 batch	Daylight Sauce (p. 112)	1 batch
Optional	Vegetables (spinach, mushrooms, broccoli, etc.)	Optional
To taste	Additional seasonings (salt, pepper, fresh or dried Italian herbs, etc.)	To taste

1. Preheat the oven at 375°F (190°C).
2. Start by preparing your zucchini lasagna noodles by slicing your zucchini as thinly as you can lengthwise.
3. Arrange your sliced zucchini on lined baking sheets (you might need two). Drizzle with your chosen fat (melt it first if solid at room temperature). Sprinkle with a bit of salt, pepper, and your favorite Italian herbs (basil and oregano work well).
4. Grill your zucchini lasagna pasta in the oven for about 15-20 minutes, turning once. You might need to cook them longer if the slices are thick. You'll know your zucchini lasagna pasta is ready when it's soft.
5. Let cool.
6. Meanwhile, stir-fry your vegetables in a bit of extra fat until cooked (optional).
7. Grease a square baking dish (8 in x 8 in or 20 cm x 20 cm).
8. Layer your zucchini lasagna noodles with the daylight sauce and optional cooked vegetables. Repeat 2-3 times until you use up all of your ingredients. You can finish with either zucchini lasagna pasta or the sauce as you like.
9. Bake in the oven (lower the temperature to 350°F/180°C) for about 15-20 minutes.
10. Serve warm. Leftovers are also good cold for breakfast the next morning.

TIPS:

- Put an interesting twist on this recipe by using sweet potatoes instead of zucchini to make your grain-free lasagna pasta. Keep in mind that the cooking time will need to be extended to at least 30-40 minutes in total to make sure your sweet potatoes slices are cooked thoroughly and easy to pierce with a fork.
- If you tolerate nightshades, you can use grilled eggplant slices as your lasagna pasta (simply slice them, drizzle with olive oil and grill in the oven until soft) and the Tomato Sauce (recipe, p. 146).
- You can easily double or triple the recipe if you want to have meals ready for the week. This recipe can also easily be frozen (whole or as individual servings) for a quick, convenient meal.
- If you tolerate cheese, especially if you can find high-quality full-fat dairy made from the milk of pastured ruminants, go ahead and add some between layers and/or on top of your lasachini!

Flavor Boosters

Caramelized Onion Jam / contains FODMAPs (onions)

Although onions are high in FODMAPs, many people can come to tolerate them well after a few months of allowing their gut to heal and rebalancing their gut flora. Caramelized onions can add a sweet but sugar-free touch to your meals. Serve them over your steak, burger or liver (recipes, pp. 102, 106 and 120).

Yields about 1 cup (250 ml):		
3-4	Medium onions, sliced or chopped	3-4
1-2 Tbsp	Ghee or butter	15-30 ml
As needed	Water	As needed
To taste	Unrefined salt	To taste

1. In a large, shallow pan, heat the ghee or butter.
2. Add the onion slices. Cook the onions at low-medium, stirring occasionally, for about 20-30 minutes. You can add water or more fat if the onions stick to the pan.
3. Once the onions are soft and thoroughly cooked (and any water fully evaporated), they should start to caramelize. Your jam will be ready once your onions are a slight golden color.
4. Season to taste and serve immediately.

TIPS:

- Prepare a larger batch and you can keep your caramelized onion jam in the fridge for at least 3-4 days… if it lasts that long!

notes:

Chimichurri

Chimichurri is an Argentinean sauce that's usually served with grilled meat. You can use it as a marinade, spread it over any kind of protein, or use it as a dip for your vegetables. It's a tasty way to add more healthy fats from olive oil and antioxidants from fresh herbs into your diet.

Yields just over 1 cup (250 ml):		
1 cup	Fresh parsley (packed)	250 ml
¼ cup	Fresh cilantro (optional)	60 ml
½ cup	Olive oil (regular or garlic-infused)	125 ml
2	Garlic cloves (if tolerated)	2
1/3 cup	Apple cider vinegar (or red wine vinegar)	80 ml
1 tsp	Unrefined salt	5 ml
To taste	Seasonings (cumin, thyme, lemon juice, paprika, etc.)	To taste

1. Put all the ingredients you want to use in a food processor or blender.
2. Blend until smooth.

TIPS:

- Chimichurri will keep in the refrigerator for about a week. If you have too much, freeze the extra in an ice trays for easy-to-thaw chimichurri cubes.

notes:

Caramelized Garlic / contains FODMAPs (garlic)

Caramelizing garlic brings out its natural sweetness. Caramelized garlic cloves can easily be squeezed out and spread on your meat or vegetables. If you're sensitive to FODMAPs, wait until your symptoms have been under control for a few months before giving this a try in the reintroduction phase. Until you tolerate FODMAPs, use FODMAP-free Garlicky Ghee (recipe, p. 162) or Garlic-Infused Oil (see *DHwRF*, p. 284) if you miss the taste of garlic.

Yields 2-3 heads of caramelized garlic:		
2-3 1-2 Tbsp	Garlic heads (not cloves—the full heads!) Olive oil	2-3 15-30 ml

1. Slice about ½ inch (1 cm) off the top of your whole garlic heads (leave the skin on).
2. Put the garlic heads on a baking sheet. Drizzle with olive oil.
3. Roast in the oven at 375°F (190°C) for about 45-60 minutes or until the garlic is soft and caramelized (slightly golden).
4. Let cool before serving.

TIPS:

• Caramelized garlic will keep in the fridge for a few days.

notes:

Herbed Ghee (or Butter) / appropriate for the elimination phase

A higher-fat diet doesn't have to be boring or smothered with unappetizing oils. Be creative with your fats and aromatize them to keep your diet varied and interesting. This herbed ghee is delicious served with any kinds of protein or vegetables.

Yields 1 cup (250 ml):		
1 cup	Ghee (recipe, p. 160)	250 ml
2-3 Tbsp	Fresh herbs, finely chopped	30-45 ml

1. In a bowl, mix your ghee (at room temperature) with the fresh herbs. Season to taste with unrefined salt (if your ghee is unsalted).
2. Keep at room temperature or in the refrigerator.

TIPS:

- If you tolerate butter, you can make herbed butter. Melt your butter, mix with the herbs and put it back in the fridge to solidify. Herbed butter, just like herbed ghee, is delicious on meat, fish or vegetables.
- Try different combinations of fresh herbs such as tarragon, thyme, parsley, oregano and rosemary.
- Pipe the herbed ghee/butter into small serving dishes for a festive look.
- You can also mix equal amounts of ghee or butter and pesto for a delicious, antioxidant-rich spread. This spread will be softer than pure ghee or butter, even if kept in the refrigerator.
- Freeze your herbed ghee/butter in an ice cube tray, and simply grab a cube or two when you need some to prepare a meal.

notes:

Crock-Pot Ghee / appropriate for the elimination phase

Ghee, or clarified butter, is a safe, dairy-free fat that you can use even during the elimination phase of the *DHwRF* protocol (unless you have a severe dairy allergy, of course). You learned how to make your own ghee on the stovetop on p. 246 of *DHwRF*, but here's an even easier way to prepare it in a slow cooker. Choose good-quality butter made from the milk of grass-fed, pastured cows for a nutritional boost of vitamins A, K_2 and E, along with other important fat-soluble nutrients.

Yields just over 4 cups (1 L):		
3 lb	Unsalted butter	1.4 kg

1. Put the butter in your slow cooker. Turn it on at a setting that will allow the butter to melt and then simmer (this could be either low or high depending on your slow cooker).
2. Let your butter simmer for about 4 hours or until it becomes golden and clear. It's completely normal for some foam and deposit to appear during this process. Your ghee is ready when you can clearly see the bottom of your slow cooker by moving the crust and foam that forms on top.
3. Turn off your slow cooker and let the ghee cool down for about an hour.
4. Place a metal colander over a large bowl and cover it with cheesecloth.
5. Pour the cooled ghee into the bowl to filter it. Careful, your ghee might still be hot! The coagulated dairy protein will stay in your cheesecloth, making your ghee dairy free.
6. Transfer your filtered ghee to Mason jars or other glass containers. Let sit at room temperature.

TIPS:

- The texture of your ghee can vary between soft and solid depending on the room temperature. Keep it in the fridge if you prefer a harder texture, or at room temperature if you like it softer.
- Don't be afraid of making big batches of ghee, since it keeps for months, even at room temperature.
- Unsalted butter is what is traditionally used to prepare ghee, but salted butter also works.
- Use ghee for cooking, add it to a vegetable purée or simply drizzle it over your vegetables.
- **Coconut ghee.** You can mix your melted ghee with an equal amount of coconut oil to create a new, versatile fat to use in your kitchen. You can even add spices and herbs for more variety. The possibilities are endless: You can make ginger ghee, cinnamon ghee, Italian ghee, or ghee with herbes de Provence. Or try the Garlicky Ghee (recipe, p. 162).
- The better the quality of the butter, the better-tasting and more nutritious your ghee will be.

Garlicky Ghee / FODMAP-free, appropriate for the elimination phase

Many garlic fans are sad to let it go, but it's important to eliminate it during the elimination phase considering its high FODMAP content. Fortunately, the FODMAPs found in garlic are water-soluble, which means that you can infuse the garlic flavor in any kind of fat to benefit from its aroma without suffering the negative side effects of its FODMAPs. This garlicky ghee can be used to cook your protein or vegetables. You can also keep it in the fridge if you prefer to use it as a spread for your meals.

Yields just over 1 cup (250 ml):		
1 cup 5-6	Ghee (recipe, p. 160) Garlic cloves	250 ml 5-6

1. Peel the garlic cloves and cut each one in half.
2. Put the garlic cloves in a small skillet with the ghee.
3. Heat at medium temperatures until the ghee starts simmering.
4. Reduce the temperature and let your ghee simmer for about 10 minutes until the garlic is soft and slightly golden. Keep the heat low to prevent the garlic from burning.
5. Let cool, strain the ghee and discard the garlic.

TIPS:

- Make a garlic purée with the caramelized garlic cloves and give it to someone who can handle FODMAPs. This purée is delicious spread on a steak or added to homemade sauces and mayonnaises.
- If you make your own ghee, you can skip a step by adding the garlic cloves directly to the butter to allow the garlic to infuse while making your ghee.
- Freeze your garlicky ghee in an ice cube tray for quick, easy use in recipes.

notes:

Creamy Ghee / appropriate for the elimination phase

Ghee is a wonderful fat to use. It provides all the essential fat-soluble nutrients found in butter (vitamins A, E and K_2, and CLAs) without any of dairy's potentially problematic compounds (casein, whey and lactose) and with a pleasant caramel taste as a bonus. This simple technique will allow you use ghee as a dip or sauce for your REAL food.

Yields just over ½ cup (125 ml):		
½ cup	Ghee	125 ml

1. Put the ghee in a medium bowl. The ghee should be at room temperature, but not liquid, for best results.
2. Whisk the soft ghee by hand for about 5 minutes until the color becomes a bit whiter and the consistency becomes airy and creamy. You can also use an electric mixer on the lowest speed for a couple of minutes or until you get the right consistency.
3. Keep your creamy ghee at room temperature or in the fridge. It will harden but will keep a creamier and lighter consistency.

TIPS:

- Add lemon juice, lemon zest, ginger, grated garlic or fresh herbs before refrigerating to pair your creamy ghee with any of your favorite meals. Or use garlic-flavored or lemon-infused ghee to make your creamy ghee.
- Have a spoonful of creamy ghee whenever you have a craving, need a little pick-me-up snack between meals, or want to end your meal with a sugar-free treat. Add cinnamon to your creamy ghee for a satisfyingly sweet but sugar-free treat. Or use it in the Cinnamon Ghee Bites (recipe, p. 76).

notes:

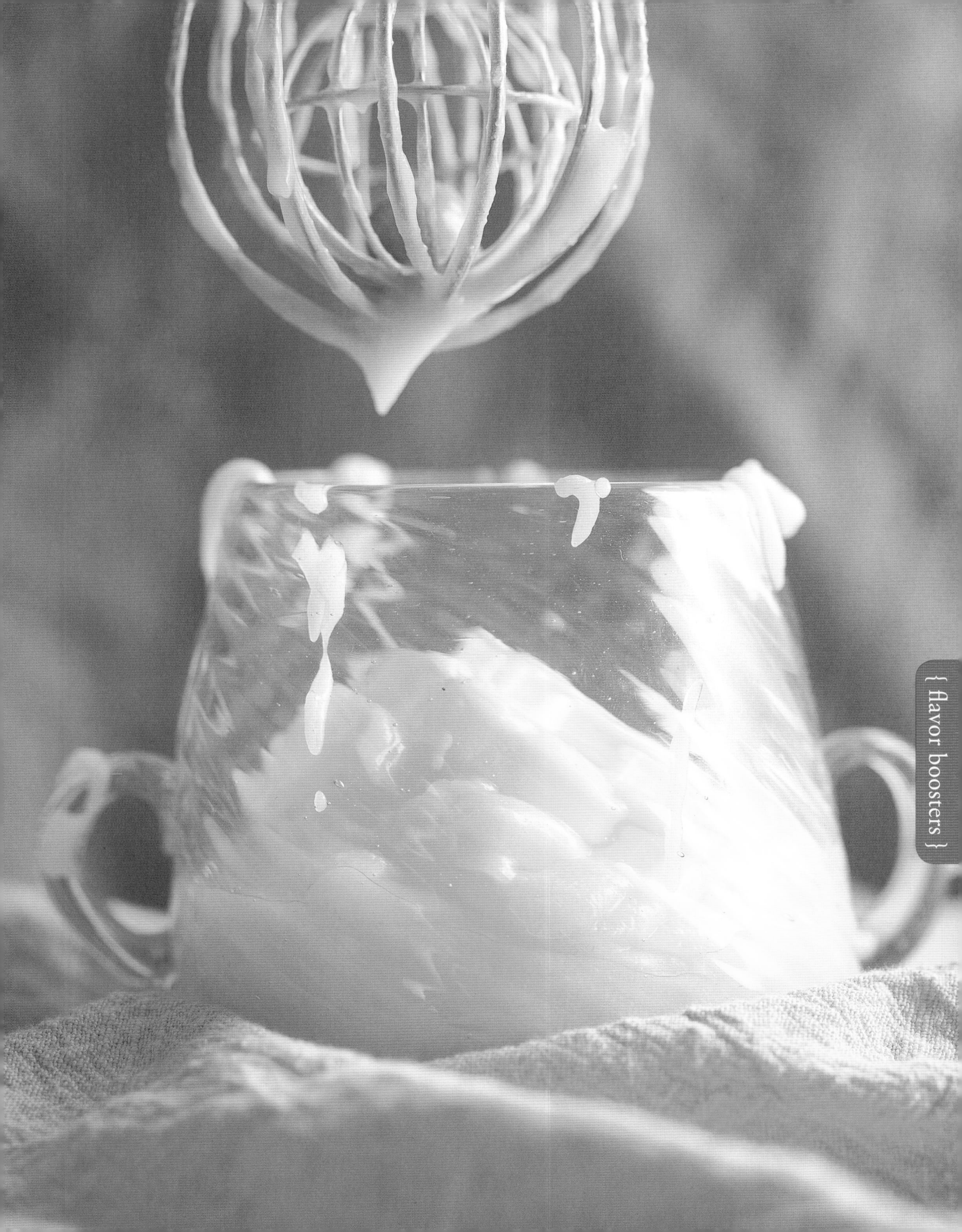

Guacamole / contains FODMAPs (avocado)

Guacamole is a great way to add more vitamin E and healthy fats to your diet. Guacamole makes a delicious dip for your veggies, meat, fish or seafood, for your grain-free burgers or wraps or you can also use it instead of mayo to prepare deviled eggs (recipe, p. 288 of *DHwRF*). If you have digestive problems, introduce avocado slowly, as it does contain some FODMAPs, so gradually to assess your individual tolerance.

Yields 1-2 cups (250-500 ml):		
1-2 To taste To taste	Avocado, ripe Lemon or lime juice Unrefined salt and other seasonings	1-2 To taste To taste

1. Peel the avocado and remove the seed.
2. Put the avocado in a bowl and mash it with a fork until you get the desired consistency. Some people like their guacamole chunkier, while others prefer it smoother.
3. Add the lemon/lime juice and seasonings to taste.
4. Eat immediately or cover tightly with plastic wrap to prevent the guacamole from coming into contact with air, as this causes browning.

TIPS:

- Use guacamole to dip your vegetables, or spread it on your protein.
- Mix equal amounts of guacamole and homemade mayonnaise in the blender to create a creamy and tasty sauce or dressing for your meat and veggies.
- Some people believe that leaving the avocado seed in the guacamole prevents it from browning. Give it a try and see for yourself!

notes:

Coconut-Asian Sauce / contains coconut milk and nuts

This Asian-inspired sauce goes well with chicken, fish and shrimp. You can also use it as a dip for your skewers, veggies or even fruits. Try it with the Asian Noodle Bowl (recipe, p. 140).

Yields 1 cup (250 ml):		
½ cup	Coconut milk (or cream if you want it thicker)	125 ml
½ cup	Almond butter	125 ml
2 Tbsp	Coconut aminos (or gluten-free tamari sauce)	30 ml
1 Tbsp	Lime juice	15 ml
½ Tbsp	Grated ginger root	7 ml
To taste	Grated garlic (if FODMAPs are tolerated)	To taste
To taste	Chili powder (if nightshades are tolerated)	To taste

1. Combine all the ingredients in a bottle or glass jar.
2. Mix by hand by putting the lid on and shaking the bottle or glass jar. You can also use a blender if you prefer.
3. Keep in the fridge for up to 5-6 days.
4. Serve cold or warm.

TIPS:

- If you don't tolerate almonds, omit the almond butter and replace it with another nut butter (macadamia nut butter, cashew butter or sunflower seed butter, for instance) or simply use more coconut milk or coconut cream.
- To make this recipe work as a **fruit dip**, simply omit the coconut aminos, lime juice, garlic, and chili powder and only use the coconut milk and nut butter. The ginger is optional. A little vanilla or unsweetened cocoa powder can help you create new varieties of fruit dips. Be creative!

notes:

Hollandaise Sauce / contains egg yolks

Hollandaise sauce is a traditional French sauce typically served over Eggs Benedict or asparagus. You can also use this sauce with fish, chicken, eggs, or any vegetables you like. This recipe should yield 1-2 servings, but you can easily double or triple the batch if you want.

Yields about ¼ cup (60 ml):		
4 Tbsp	Ghee or butter	60 ml
2	Egg yolks	2
2 Tbsp	Cold water	30 ml
1 Tbsp	Lemon juice	15 ml
To taste	Unrefined salt	To taste
To taste	Seasonings	To taste

1. In a small double boiler over low heat, whisk the egg yolks and water together until their color becomes paler and their consistency smoother and creamier. Make sure the water in the double boiler is only barely simmering if you don't want to end up with scrambled eggs.
2. Continue whisking and very slowly add the melted fat (ghee or butter) in a stream. Ask the help of someone else to pour the oil if needed. The oil should be poured slowly enough to allow the egg yolk to emulsify (thicken) with the oil.
3. Add the lemon juice, salt and other seasonings to taste.
4. Serve immediately.

TIPS:

- You can also replace the fat with coconut oil, light-tasting olive oil, macadamia oil or avocado oil.
- Add lemon zest and different herbs (basil, thyme, oregano, rosemary, parsley) to change the flavors of your Hollandaise sauce.
- You can easily double the batch if you need more, but don't try to make extra for leftovers. Hollandaise sauce should be served within 2 hours or it will start to separate and look very unappetizing.

notes:

Raccourci Ratatouille / contains FODMAPs and nightshades

Ratatouille is a French vegetable stew usually made with eggplants, tomatoes and other vegetables. The technique used for the original recipe can be quite complicated and time-consuming but I find that this recipe is the perfect compromise to save your precious time while still adding rich flavors to your diet. Raccourci actually means "shortcut" in French. This recipe makes a tasty base on which you can serve eggs or any kind of leftover meat. Drizzle with olive oil for extra healthy fats.

Yields 3-4 cups (0.75-1L) of ratatouille:		
3-4 Tbsp	Olive oil	45-60 ml
1	Onion, diced	1
1-2	Eggplant, medium	1-2
1-2 cups	Tomatoes, diced (fresh or canned)	250-500 ml
1-2	Zucchini	1-2
To taste	Unrefined salt and seasonings	To taste

1. Cut all of your vegetables into small cubes.
2. Heat the olive oil under medium heat in a large saucepan.
3. Add the onions, eggplant and zucchini.
4. Cook under medium temperature for about 20-30 minutes, or until completely tender. Stir occasionally and add more oil or water if necessary to prevent the vegetables from sticking at the bottom of the saucepan.
5. Add the diced tomato and cook 10-15 minutes more. Turn off the heat and season to taste.

TIPS:

- The Raccourci Ratatouille can keep for 5-6 days in the fridge. You can also freeze extras for later use.
- Add other vegetables like yellow squash and bell peppers if you like. These vegetables are all included in a classic ratatouille.
- Ratatouille can also be served as a side dish.
- You can replace the diced tomatoes with the same amount of Tomato Sauce (recipe, p. 146).
- Omit the onion to make this recipe lower in FODMAPs.
- If you aren't short on time and don't need to take a raccourci (shortcut), you can carefully layer the sliced vegetables in a baking dish, drizzle with olive oil, season to taste, and bake in the oven at 350°F (180°C) for about 45 minutes, or until cooked.

Grass-Fed Tallow / appropriate for the elimination diet

Tallow not only imparts a wonderful, rich flavor to your foods, but it also adds a nutritional boost to your meals—especially if you make the tallow from the fat of grass-fed cows. You may be able to find tallow at your butcher's store or the local farmers market, but it's also surprisingly easy to make at home. Unfortunately, butchers and farmers often throw away their beef fat since most people don't want it, so be sure to ask them to keep it for you. You can keep your beef fat frozen until you're ready to make your tallow.

Yields about 4-8 cups or 1-2 L:

2-4 lb	Beef fat, ideally from a grass-fed animal	1-2 kg

1. Cut the beef fat into large chunks. Throw everything in a slow cooker.
2. Set your slow cooker at the lowest setting for 8-10 hours. This step is called the "rendering" of your fat.
3. Let your tallow cool for 1-2 hours before draining in a fine colander. If your colander has larger holes, place some cheesecloth on top. Discard the crispy bits.
4. Transfer the melted tallow to Mason jars or other glass containers. Your tallow will turn white as it solidifies.

TIPS:

- Tallow can be kept at room temperature for a whole year. Make sure it is stored away from light and oxygen. You might need to remove a thin top layer if it becomes oxidized (the color will change), but the rest of your tallow will still be good.
- Tallow is an excellent cooking fat for your meat, vegetables, and even baked goods like grain-free muffins and cookies (look at the recipe master list on p. 23 to find healthy ideas to use your tallow).
- **Lard.** The same rendering process can be used with pork fat to make lard. Just make sure to remove the lard rendered every couple hours to prevent it from burning.

notes:

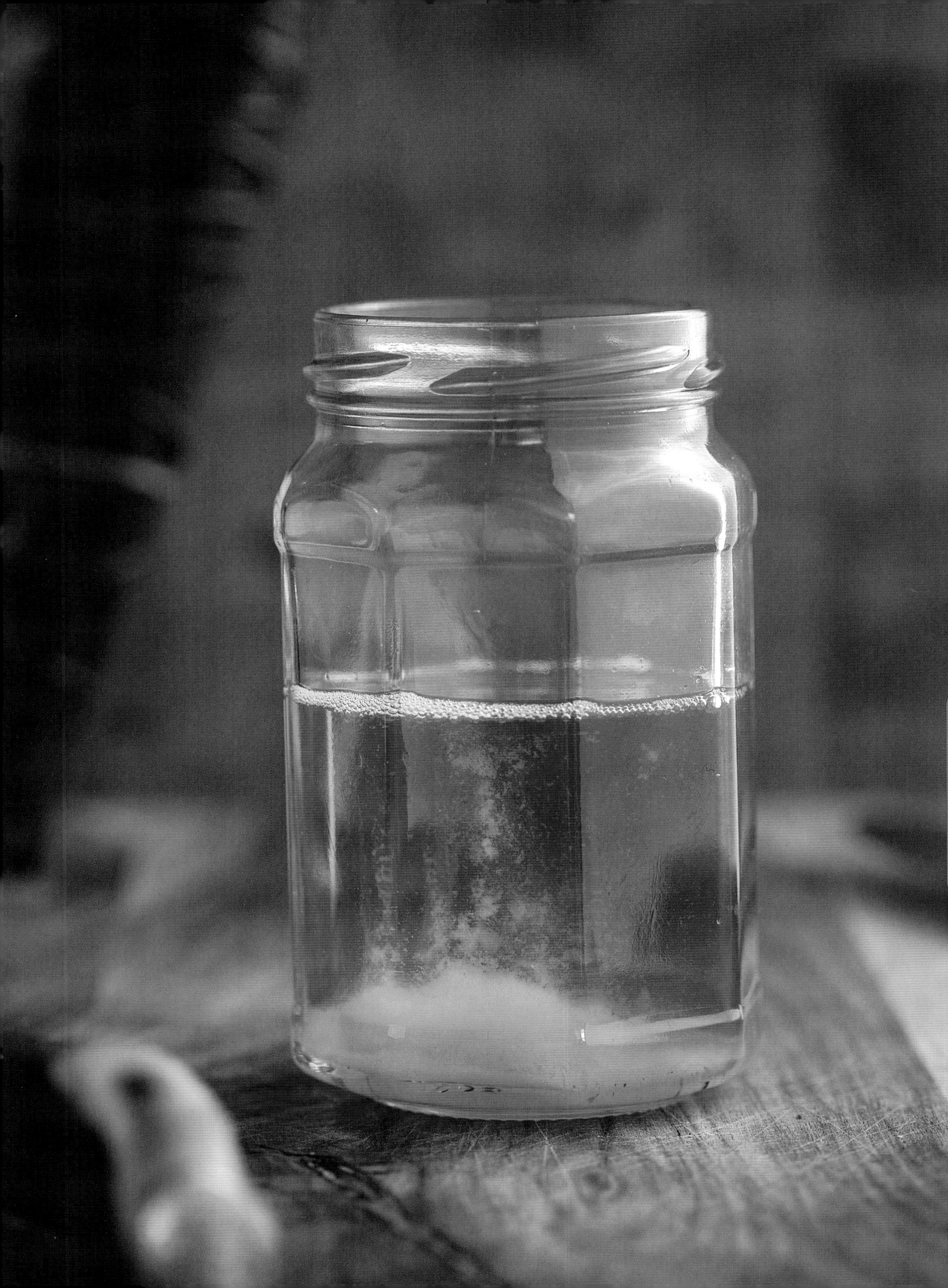

Roasted Bone Broth / appropriate for the elimination phase

Roasting bones, as you did with the Mellow Marrow (recipe, p. 30), can give your homemade bone broth more depth and flavor. Homemade bone broth supplies many important nutrients that you can't get anywhere else to help you heal and seal your gut. Eating it as often as you can, ideally daily, will help you optimize your digestive health more quickly. Don't fall for the convenience of commercial bone broths, though, because they're usually made with cheap artificial ingredients, often including wheat and MSG that could be problematic for your digestive system.

Yields 4-8 servings:		
1-2 lb	Bones	0.5-1 kg
Enough to cover	Water	Enough to cover
2-4 Tbsp	Vinegar (apple cider or white vinegar)	30-60 ml
To taste	Seasonings	To taste
As tolerated	Vegetables (carrots, onions, celery, etc.)	As tolerated

1. Place your roasted bones (unroasted bones or chicken carcass work well too) in your slow cooker.
2. Add the vinegar, seasonings and vegetables as desired.
3. Cover with water.
4. Set your slow cooker to low and leave simmering for 6-24 hours. You can also make your homemade bone broth in a big pot on the stove if you don't have a slow cooker.
5. Turn off the heat and let cool down 1-2 hours before draining.
6. Store your homemade bone broth in Mason jars or glass containers. It will keep for up to 5 days in the fridge.

TIPS:

- Don't use onions or garlic if you're sensitive to FODMAPs. Even if you drain them from the broth itself, their water-soluble FODMAPs will remain in the broth.
- You can also freeze your bone broth for 3-6 months and thaw as needed. When freezing your bone broth, make sure to leave some space to allow room for fluid expansion (otherwise your jars will explode in your freezer!). I also avoid tightening the lid on my Mason jars until my bone broth is frozen, just in case…!

notes:

Herb-Infused Oil / appropriate for the elimination diet

Infusing oil is a simple way to add more flavors to your homemade mayonnaise, salad dressings and marinades. You can also drizzle your herb-infused oil over your meals for extra healthy and tasty fats.

Yields about 1 bottle:	
One A few sprigs Enough to fill the bottle	Glass bottle Herbs (rosemary, basil, oregano, thyme, sage, cilantro, tarragon, chives, parsley, etc.) Extra-virgin olive oil, avocado oil or macadamia oil

1. Add a few sprigs of herbs (one kind only or a combination) to a glass bottle. If your herbs are fresh, it might be better to dry them first by leaving them under the sun for several hours or in a dehydrator (to prevent spoiling your herbs with the growth of unwelcomed bacteria). If you still decide to use fresh herbs, wash them thoroughly and pat them dry before placing them in the bottle to avoid introducing any water into your oil. You can also put them in the oven for a couple of hours at the lowest temperature to get rid of the surface water as a precaution.
2. Fill the bottle with your extra-virgin oil, using a fennel if necessary. Seal tight. If your glass bottle is clear, you can wrap a paper around to protect it from light.
3. Let infuse at room temperature, away from light and heat, for 2-3 weeks.
4. When ready, use your herb-infused oil to add a boost of flavor and healthy fats to your meals.

TIPS

- Do not use your Herb Infused Oil for cooking because these oils are relatively fragile. Use Herbed Ghee instead (recipe, p. 158).
- You can use your herb-infused oils to make frozen herb cubes (recipe, p. 228) to preserve it longer.

notes:

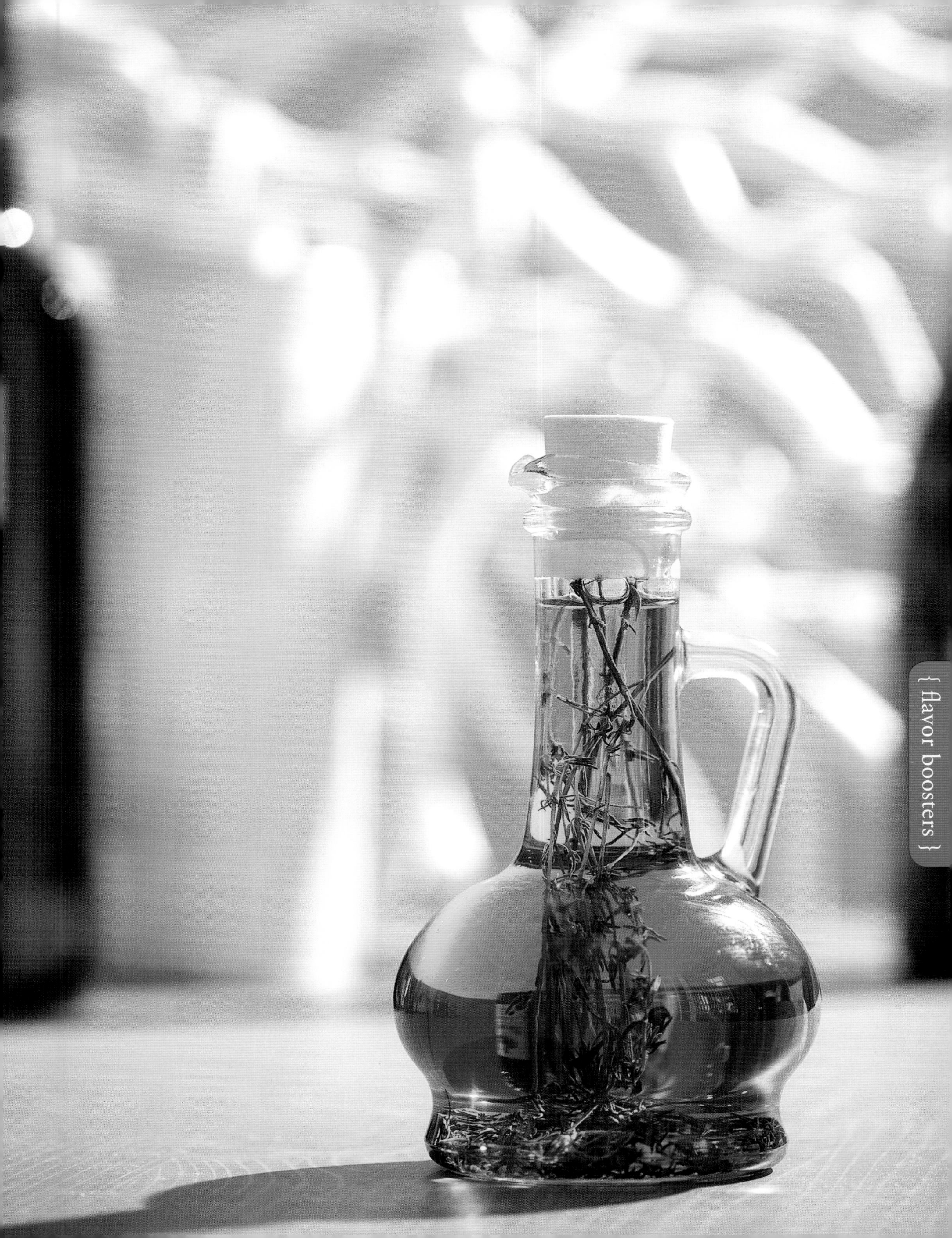

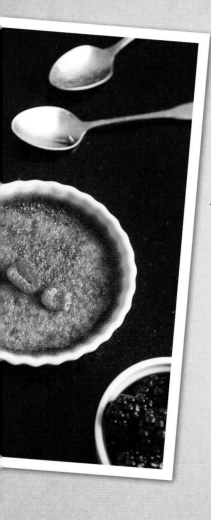

Treats

Meringue Cookies / contains eggs

Do you miss cookies? Meringues are a great way to satisfy that craving without the need for flour, nuts or even sugar! All you really need is one ingredient: egg whites. Although these cookies may be a bit more difficult to prepare if you've never beaten an egg white, it's easy to get the hang of.

Yields 12 meringue cookies:	
4	Egg whites, at room temperature
To taste	Vanilla extract and/or cinnamon

1. In a large mixing bowl, beat the egg whites at high speed until thick and glossy (about 5 minutes).
2. Add the vanilla extract or other optional seasonings and mix gently.
3. Drop tablespoons of the meringue mixture on a lined baking sheet.
4. Bake at 175°F (80°C) for about 90 minutes (the purpose is to dry the meringue cookies rather than cook them).

TIPS:

- **Add more flavors!** You can add about ½ cup (125 ml) chopped roasted nut, ¼ cup (60 ml) unsweetened cocoa powder, ½ cup (125 ml) unsweetened dried coconut or ¼ cup (60 ml) of puréed strawberries or raspberries. Sweeten to taste with a bit of melted honey or maple syrup if tolerated.
- **Trouble beating your egg whites?** Make sure you use a clean bowl and whisks free of fatty residues to beat your egg whites. Any traces of egg yolks or fat could prevent the egg whites from expanding in volume. Allowing your egg whites to be at room temperature by leaving them on the counter for 30-45 minutes before starting this recipe can also help you get more volume when beating your egg whites.
- **What should you do with the yolks?** The yolk is the most nutritious part of the egg, so please don't throw it away! Use your yolks in the Creamy Salad Dressing (recipe, p. 98) and Crème Brûlée (recipe, p. 198), or throw them in your Bananaoatmeal (recipe, p. 28), Speedy Recovery Soup (recipe, p. 134), or Energy Tea Latte (recipe, p. 208). You can also use two egg yolks to replace each whole egg when making the Faux Muffins (recipe, p. 66), the Against-the-Grain Cookies (recipe, p. 196) or the Banana Muffins (recipe, p. 88).

notes:

Creamy Cream-Free Ice Cream / contains coconut and raspberries

This refreshing treat is perfect to satisfy a sweet tooth. You can use other frozen fruits, as tolerated, to vary the flavors and sweeten with a little bit of honey or maple syrup if desired.

Yields 1 serving:		
¼-½ cup	Coconut milk	60-125 ml
¼-½ cup	Frozen raspberries	60-125 ml

1. Put the frozen raspberries in a small bowl.
2. Add just enough coconut milk to cover the raspberries.
3. Use a fork to mash the fruits into the coconut milk until you get a thicker ice cream-like consistency. Add more or less coconut milk to get the desired consistency.
4. Serve immediately!

TIPS:

- Replace the frozen raspberries with avocado. Add vanilla extract if desired. Blend until smooth and freeze for about an hour to get green ice cream!
- Use a food processor or blender to mix the frozen fruits and coconut milk if you want a smoother texture.
- **Chocolate ice cream.** Add unsweetened cocoa powder, chunks of dark chocolate and/or unsweetened dried coconut for a chocolate version. Sweeten to taste with 1-2 tsp (5-10 ml) of coconut sugar, maple syrup or honey. You can also add almond butter or whole nuts for extra texture.
- **Avoid thickeners!** Make sure your coconut milk does not contain guar gum or other thickeners, as they might irritate your digestive system. If you can't find any, make your own Coconut Milk (recipe, p. 226).

notes:

Banacado / contains banana and/or avocado

This creamy frozen treat is not only tasty, but it's filled with good-for-you nutrients like healthy fats, vitamin E and other antioxidants. Yes, desserts are not necessarily empty calories if they're made with REAL food. Like most other recipes in this cookbook, this recipe is highly customizable. Have fun with it and mix and match your favorite ingredients to create different banacado variations.

Yields 1-2 servings:		
Basic	1 medium ½	Banana, roughly chopped Avocado, roughly chopped
Optional (choose one or create your own version!)	A handful 1-2 squares 2 Tbsp (30 ml) 2-3 Tbsp 1 Tbsp (15 ml) A few drops	Frozen or fresh raspberries Dark chocolate, chopped Dried coconut, unsweetened Grated apples with a dash of cinnamon and nutmeg Lime juice Vanilla extract

1. Put the chopped banana and avocado in the freezer for a few hours, or until completely frozen.
2. Put in a food processor or blender and process until smooth.
3. Add the optional ingredients of your choice, if desired.
4. Enjoy your banacado immediately!

TIPS:

- You can also store your banacado in the freezer. Simply put it back in the food processor to make it creamy again if it hardens too much.
- Instead of using both avocado and banana, you can use either one of these ingredients, as tolerated.
- Add coconut milk to make your banacado less thick.
- Sweeten with honey or maple syrup, and add nut butter, whole nuts, unsweetened dried coconut or unsweetened cocoa powder (as tolerated) to create new banacado varieties.

notes:

Baked Pear / contains coconut and FODMAPs (pears)

Baked fruit is easier to digest than raw fruit. Baked pears make a good snack or treat that everyone can enjoy when having a family dinner or eating with friends. Pears are usually not recommended for people with fructose malabsorption because of their high fructose (FODMAPs) content, but after a few months of healing your gut and correcting your gut flora, you might be able to tolerate gradually larger amounts.

Yields 1 serving:			
1 medium	Pear	1 medium	
1-2 Tbsp	Coconut butter	15-30 ml	
To taste	Vanilla (optional)	To taste	

1. Peel the pear. This step is optional, but it can make the pear easier to digest if you're still at the beginning of your journey toward better digestive health.
2. Core the pear, making sure to remove all the seeds.
3. In a small bowl, mix the coconut butter with a few drops of vanilla extract. You can also use vanilla seeds instead.
4. Fill the inside of the pear with the coconut butter mixture.
5. Bake in the oven at 350°F (180°C) for about 45 minutes or until soft when pierced with a fork.

TIPS:

- Coconut butter is sometimes also called coconut cream concentrate or coconut manna. It's not the same as coconut oil.
- Apples and peaches work just as well for this recipe.
- You can poach the pear in water and vanilla for about 30 minutes to shorten the baking time. Add the filling after the pears are poached.
- Make many baked pears at once and reheat leftovers as needed.
- Add nuts, nut butter, honey or maple syrup to the coconut butter filling if desired.

notes:

Grilled Fruit Kebabs / contains fruits

You can enhance the natural sweetness and flavors of fruits by grilling them. Cooking also make them easier to digest. Choose fruits you tolerate and keep the quantities reasonable if you are sensitive to carbohydrates. This recipe is super simple but very fun to make. It's perfect for summer and makes a healthy but fancy treat!

Each ½ cup (125 ml) of fruits yields about 1-2 kebabs:	
A few slices of each	Fruits (pineapple, peaches, banana, kiwi, strawberries, nectarines, plums, apples, pears, cantaloupe, mango, etc.)
Optional	Coconut Whipped Cream (recipe, p. 192)

1. Cut your fruits into slices or cubes of similar thickness.
2. Thread on a skewer.
3. Grill over medium heat for about 5 minutes on each side.
4. Serve warm on their own or with the coconut whipped cream as a dip.

TIPS:

- Dip in coconut milk, Coconut Whipped Cream (recipe, p. 192) or melted chocolate, drizzle with honey or maple syrup, or sprinkle with unsweetened dried coconut or cinnamon if desired.
- If you have leftovers, combine the extra grilled fruits with coconut milk or Coconut Yogurt (recipe, p. 214).
- You can also use leftover grilled fruits to make a salsa to accompany chicken or fish. All you need to do is dice the grilled fruits finely and call it a salsa!

notes:

Coconut Whipped Cream / contains coconut; dairy-free

   If you tolerate coconut, you can use it to create a variety of dairy-free, grain-free treats. This coconut whipped cream works great with fruit, with a grain-free cookie or muffin, or on its own.

Yields about 1 cup (250 ml):	
1 can	Coconut milk

1. Put the coconut milk in the refrigerator overnight.
2. The next day, flip the coconut milk can upside down and open it up.
3. The top of the flipped can will be coconut water and the bottom, coconut cream. Drain the water and put it aside. You won't need it for this recipe.
4. Scoop out the coconut cream and put it in a large bowl.
5. Whip the coconut cream with a mixer, at high speed, until creamy and fluffy.

TIPS:

- Choose coconut milk without guar gum or other thickeners to prevent unpleasant digestive side effects.
- Sweeten with a little honey or maple syrup if desired.
- Your whipped coconut cream can keep for about a week in the fridge, but it will probably be all gone before then! If it hardens, re-whip it to loosen it up.
- Don't discard the coconut water. You can use it in soups, stews, or smoothies, or drink it on its own. Coconut water is rich in electrolytes and therefore makes a very good rehydration fluid when you're sick or after a workout.

notes:

Coconut Fudge / contains coconut

   This coconut fudge recipe is very similar to the Coconut Bark (recipe, p. 84), with slightly different ratios of coconut ingredients to make it creamier. As with Coconut Bark, it's a good idea to keep this fudge in the fridge (or freezer), and grab some to satisfy your sweet tooth whenever needed. The natural sweetness of coconut lets you keep this treat entirely sugar-free.

Yields about 12 servings:		
1 cup	Coconut butter	250 ml
½ cup	Unsweetened dried shredded coconut	125 ml
To taste	Vanilla extract	To taste

1. Melt the coconut butter by putting it in the microwave or letting your glass jar of coconut butter sit in hot water for a few minutes.
2. Mix all the ingredients of the recipe together.
3. Pour into a Pyrex bowl (or individual silicone muffin cups).
4. Refrigerate until firm and cut into squares.

TIPS:

- Add lemon zest, honey, maple syrup, dried fruits, nuts or unsweetened cocoa powder as tolerated.
- You can boost the coconut flavor of this recipe by first grilling the shredded coconut in a non-adhesive skillet under medium heat for a few minutes, stirring regularly to prevent burning, until slightly golden.

notes:

Against-the-Grain Cookies / contains eggs, coconut and/or nuts

Coconut flour and nut flour are great ingredients that you can use to prepare a variety of grain-free recipes to replace your old favorites. They both work very well but result in slightly different tastes and textures. Almond flour can almost always be used one-for-one in most recipes, but be aware that coconut flour is very different and usually requires more liquids and protein (eggs) to make a satisfying end product. Experiment with both to decide which option works best for you. Or if you're intolerant to nuts like I am, go for the safer coconut flour. Both options are so delicious that you can serve them to your friends or family members and no one will know that they are completely grain-free!

Type	Yields about 12 cookies:			Yields about 20-24 cookies:		
	Coconut flour base			**Almond flour base**		
Basic	⅔ cup	Coconut oil, butter or ghee	160 ml	¾ cup	Coconut oil, butter or ghee	175 ml
	⅓ cup	Coconut flour	80 ml	3 cups	Almond flour	750 ml
	3	Eggs	3	2	Eggs	2
	1 tsp	Baking soda (optional)	5 ml	1 tsp	Baking soda (optional)	5 ml
	Dash	Unrefined salt	Dash	Dash	Unrefined salt	Dash
	1 tsp	Vanilla	5 ml	1 tsp	Vanilla	5 ml
Optional	¼ cup	Unsweetened cocoa				60 ml
	¼ cup	Maple syrup or honey				60 ml
	½ cup	Dried fruits, nuts (raw or roasted), unsweetened dried coconut (raw or toasted) or dark chocolate chunks				125 ml

1. Melt your chosen fat and transfer to a large mixing bowl.
2. Add the rest of the ingredients and combine until you get a smooth batter. If using the coconut flour base, let rest about 5 minutes to allow time for the coconut flour to absorb the liquids.
3. Form the dough into cookies on a lined baking sheet.
4. Bake in the oven at 350°F (180°C) for about 12-15 minutes, or until the dough is set and the edges are slightly golden.

TIPS:

- **Make your own almond flour.** Almond flour and other nut flours can be expensive—so make your own! All you need to do is to process raw nuts in a food processor for 2-3 minutes until you get a coarse, flour-like consistency. Making your own coconut flour is not as easy, so it's easier to just buy it. And you generally need a lot less of it than you do almond flour, so it's worth the investment.
- **Add vegetables!** Another way to add a new twist to your cookies is by adding ⅓-⅔ cup (80-160 ml) of grated carrots or zucchini.

Coconut Crème Brûlée / dairy-free; contains egg yolks, coconut and sugar

Crème brûlée is one of my all-time favorite desserts, and one of my mother's specialties. When I took dairy out of my diet, my mother worked on developing a dairy-free, lower-sugar version that I could tolerate. This coconut crème brûlée makes a very elegant dessert, and the creaminess of coconut will fool everyone into thinking that it's the real, classical French version with a coconut bonus. The traditional recipe has at least double the amount of sugar used here. Fortunately, the natural sweetness of coconut will allow you to use less sugar without compromising the taste. Merci maman!

Yields 6-8 servings:		
1/4 cup	Coconut sugar	60 ml
8	Large egg yolks	8
2 cups	Coconut cream	500 ml
½ cup	Unsweetened dried shredded coconut	125 ml
1	Vanilla bean	1

1. Preheat oven to 325°F (160°C).
2. Meanwhile, beat the egg yolks, gradually adding the sugar, until smooth.
3. Scrape the seeds from the vanilla beans and add them to the egg yolk mixture.
4. In a small pan, heat the coconut cream until almost simmering.
5. Slowly pour the heated coconut cream to the egg yolk mixture, whisking vigorously.
6. Incorporate the unsweetened dried coconut.
7. Pour the crème brûlée mixture into 6-8 ramekins.
8. Place the ramekins in a baking pan and add enough hot water to the pan for it to come about halfway up the sides of the ramekins.
9. Bake for 40-45 minutes or until the cremes brûlées are set on the edges but still jiggly in the center.
10. Allow the cremes brûlées to cool down for about 30 minutes before removing the ramekins from the baking pan. Refrigerate for at least 2 hours.
11. Before serving, you can add about ½-1 tsp (2-5 ml) of coconut sugar on top of each crème brûlée and use a torch to melt and caramelize the sugar to form a delicious, crispy top. Make sure that the sugar layer is very thin and uniform. Be careful because coconut sugar tends to burn faster compared to granulated sugar. If you don't have a torch, simply place your cremes brûlées on the highest grill under broil for about 2 minutes, and watch them closely to prevent burning.

TIPS:

- Coconut cream is higher in fat than coconut milk because it doesn't have added water. If you can't find coconut cream, you can make your own by refrigerating coconut milk overnight (you'll probably need 2 cans). Then, open the cans but use only the solidified coconut cream that forms at the top of the can and discard the coconut water that settles at the bottom (you can also drink it, or use it for smoothies or soups). Coconut milk will also work for this recipe, but the end result won't be as rich and creamy.
- **Chocolate version.** Add ¼ cup (60 ml) of unsweetened cocoa powder for a chocolate version or serve your crème brûlée with fresh fruit to give a new twist to this recipe.
- You can also replace the coconut sugar with organic granulated cane sugar to make it easier to form a crispy top layer, especially if using a torch. Granulated sugar is less likely to burn because of its granular shape.
- **What should you do with the extra egg whites?** Try the Meringue Cookies (recipe, p. 182)!

Clean Mendiants / contains cocoa powder, nuts and/or dried fruits

Mendiants are a traditional French chocolate disk stuffed with nuts and dried fruits. The word "mendiant" translates to "mendicant"—and you may in fact find many people begging for them! We can make these mendiants super "clean" by using homemade chocolate! You can also use a good-quality dark chocolate that you like, but making it from scratch is a great way to avoid the soy lecithin and flavorings, as well as control the amount of sugar in the recipe. And they're pretty enough to give as a present!

Yields about 8 oz (250 g):			
Base	2 Tbsp ½ cup	Cocoa powder, unsweetened Cocoa butter, coconut oil or unsalted butter	30 ml 125 ml
Optional	1 Tbsp A few drops 2-3 Tbsp 2-3 Tbsp 2-3 Tbsp 2-3 Tbsp To taste	Coconut sugar or maple syrup (optional) Vanilla Dried shredded coconut, unsweetened Dried fruits (cranberries, raisins, apricots, cherries, goji berries, etc.) Nuts (almonds, pistachios, macadamia, hazelnuts, etc.) Bacon, cooked and chopped Seasonings (fleur de sel, pink peppercorns, mint leaves, etc.)	15 ml A few drops 30-45 ml 30-45 ml 30-45 ml 30-45 ml To taste

1. Melt your chosen fat (ideally in a double boiler) and mix with the unsweetened cocoa powder.
2. Add the desired optional ingredients. If you want to make different varieties, separate the chocolate mixture into 2 or 3 small bowls and add different combinations of optional ingredients to each one of them. For example, you could have vanilla; coconut and cranberry; bacon and fleur de sel; almond and dried cherry; or pink peppercorn mendiants. Use your imagination!
3. Pour small circles of your mendiant mixture on a lined baking sheet. Alternatively, simply pour a thin layer of the mendiant mixture into individual silicone muffin liners.
4. Put your baking sheets or individual muffin liners in the fridge or freezer for 10-15 minutes until set.
5. Carefully remove your mendiants from the lined baking sheet or silicon muffin liners.
6. Transfer your mendiants to a storage container and keep them in the fridge or freezer to prevent them from melting.
7. When ready to eat, simply take a few out. Eat right away or bring to room temperature (if you can resist the temptation long enough).

TIPS:

- Instead of using vanilla extract, you can simply scrape the insides of vanilla beans and use vanilla bean paste in this recipe.
- **Make your own chocolate bars!** You can use this same recipe to make bark or chocolate bars. Mix all the desired ingredients and pour the chocolate mixture, in the desired shape, on a parchment paper. Let set. For barks, simply break pieces of chocolate and store in a nice container for whenever you have a chocolate craving.
- **Chocolate cups.** You can also use a simple mixture of cocoa powder and healthy fats to make chocolate cups. Line a muffin pan with paper or silicon liners and use a brush to coat the inside of the liners evenly. Make sure the layer is thick enough that it will hold once set. If the chocolate is too liquid to coat a thick layer, simply let it set and brush a second layer to make it thicker, then let set in the fridge. Carefully remove the liners and serve your chocolate cups with fresh fruit, the Creamy Cream-Free Ice Cream (recipe, p. 184) or the Banacado (recipe, p. 186).

Watermelon Snow / contains FODMAPs (watermelon)

This recipe is super simple, and the refreshing texture and coldness of this watermelon snow makes it a perfect treat anytime of the day. This treat is great sprinkled with frozen blueberries to satisfy occasional post-dinner cravings.

Yields 6-8 servings:	
Basic	Half of a watermelon
Optional	Blueberries, frozen

1. Carefully cut your watermelon into big chunks of 1-2 in (2-5 cm) in size. Discard the skin.
2. Line a baking sheet with parchment paper. Place the watermelon chunks on it, leaving a bit of space between each of them (or else the watermelon will freeze as a giant block).
3. Put the watermelon in the freezer for at least 1-2 hours or until completely frozen.
4. Put watermelon chunks in a strong blender or food processor and process until it looks like pink snow. You might need to repeat this step a few times until you've used all of your frozen watermelon chunks.
5. Scoop out the watermelon snow and serve immediately.
6. Place any extra in a container and store in the freezer.
7. Serve your watermelon snow with frozen blueberries if desired.

TIPS:

- Experiment with different varieties of melon to create different flavors.
- If your watermelon snow sticks together after staying in the freezer for too long, scoop it out and process it again in your blender until you obtain a light texture again.
- **Sugar-free watermelon slush.** Mix watermelon snow with cold water for a refreshing, sugar-free slush.

notes:

Drinks

Good-for-the-Tummy Tea / contains coconut milk and sugar

If you want something warm to drink to soothe your tummy, try this recipe. Make sure you choose coconut milk that is free of guar gum or other thickeners that can actually make your digestive problems worse. A clean coconut milk should only contain coconut and water. If you can't find any, make your own (recipe, p. 226). Coconut milk has antimicrobial properties, and contains healthy MCT fats that provide quick energy. Turmeric is well known for its anti-inflammatory properties, and ginger can help improve your digestion.

Yields 1-2 servings:		
1 cup	Coconut milk (ideally without thickeners)	250 ml
½ tsp	Turmeric	2 ml
1 tsp	Fresh ginger root, grated	5 ml
½-1 tsp each	Cinnamon, nutmeg or cardamom (optional)	2-5 ml each
½ tsp	Honey, maple syrup or coconut sugar	2 ml

1. In a small skillet, warm the coconut milk.
2. Once warmed, add all the other ingredients and whisk until homogenous. Taste and adjust the seasoning to suit your taste preferences.
3. You can either pour the tea directly into a mug or filter it using a tea filter if you want to remove the grated ginger.
4. Enjoy!

TIPS:

- You can also make a larger batch of this tea to keep in the fridge and reheat as needed.
- If you don't tolerate coconut milk, a simple tea made by pouring boiling water over freshly grated ginger root is another good way to soothe your tummy and help your digestion. Or try the Energy Tea Latte (recipe, p. 208).

notes:

Energy Tea Latte / appropriate for the elimination diet; caffeine-free and dairy-free

This energy tea latte is the perfect healthy substitute for coffee, pop or energy drinks. Rooibos is a South African plant that means "red bush." Tea made from its leaves is naturally free of caffeine, and the addition of coconut oil can help give you a quick energy boost. The coconut oil also gives your tea a smooth, creamy texture that resembles a latte, but without any dairy!

Original version (appropriate for elimination diet)

Yields 1-2 cups (250-500 ml):		
1-2 cups	Rooibos tea, freshly brewed	250-500 ml
1-2 Tbsp	Coconut oil or ghee	15-30 ml

1. Pour your freshly brewed rooibos tea in a blender. Be careful if still warm/hot.
2. Add the coconut oil or ghee.
3. Put the lid on your blender and process until homogenous and foamy.
4. Enjoy!

Creamy Chai Tea Latte (contains coconut butter and spices)

Yields 2 cups (500 ml):		
2 cups	Rooibos tea, freshly brewed	500 ml
1-2 Tbsp	Coconut butter	15-30 ml
¼ tsp	Turmeric, powder	1 ml
¼ tsp	Nutmeg, powder	1 ml
½ tsp	Cinnamon, powder	2 ml
¼ tsp	Vanilla extract	1 ml

1. Follow the same instructions as for the original version. Adjust the spices to your personal preference. Some of the spices in this Energy Chai Tea Latte have anti-inflammatory properties and can help soothe your tummy.
2. Enjoy immediately! Make sure you shake if (if you have a safe lid) or stir it once in a while because the seasonings tend to sink at the bottom.

TIPS:

- Experiment with different types of teas and herbal teas.
- If the oil separates from the tea, which can happen if your tea latte is left undisturbed for too long, simply pour it back into your blender and process until smooth again.
- You can use unsalted butter or coconut butter instead of coconut oil.
- Drinking this healthy-fat-enriched tea is a great way to sneak more calories into your diet if you're underweight or have difficulty eating enough to nourish your body.
- For a delicious foam on top of your latte, add a raw egg yolk (only if you trust your egg source, though) to the other ingredients when blending your tea. Egg yolks from pastured fowl will also give you a nutritional boost by supplying extra vitamins A, D, and E, B vitamins, and the good-for-your-eyes antioxidants lutein and zeaxanthin.
- **Healing boost.** Add extra protein and gut-healing nutrients to your energy tea latte by sprinkling 1 Tbsp (15 ml) of gelatin (ideally from grass-fed and pastured animals like the Great Lakes brand) and 500-1,000 mg of L-glutamine powder (or the powder from 1-2 capsules). Just make sure you sprinkle the gelatin in a very thin layer and let it absorb water for a few minutes to avoid lumps. The L-glutamine dissolves very easily. Blend until dissolved.
- For a refreshing cool drink, pour your energy tea latte over ice or simply let it sit at room temperature or in the fridge for a while.

Virgin Cocktail / contains carbonated water; alcohol-free

Going to a party or special occasion and don't want to be the only one abstaining from a special drink? The good news is that you can easily treat yourself to a fancy drink without alcohol. After you've been following the *DHwRF* protocol for a few months, you might be able to occasionally tolerate small amounts of alcohol (ideally free of gluten and sugar, like tequila or cider). However, if your digestion is not yet under control, it might be best to stick to this alcohol-free cocktail to avoid further damaging your gut and slowing your healing.

Yields 1 serving:		
½ - 1 cup	Carbonated water or Kombucha (recipe, p. 218)	125-250 ml
2-3	Ice cubes	2-3
Splash	Lemon or lime juice	Splash
1-3	Lemon or lime wedges	1-3

1. Put a few ice cubes at the bottom of a fancy cocktail or wine glass.
2. Cover with carbonated water.
3. Add a splash of lemon or lime juice.
4. Decorate with a few lemon or lime wedges.
5. Cheers! Santé! ¡Salud! Prost!

TIPS:

- Instead of the lime or lemon wedges, add a few slices of fresh fruit or a small handful of frozen berries to infuse your alcohol-free cocktail and make it look even more elegant and refreshing.
- **Juice it up!** If you can handle small amounts of natural fruit sugars, you can even mix your carbonated water with equal parts of unsweetened fruit juice to add a bit of color and flavor.
- **Add a splash of green!** If you don't do well with either carbonated water or kombucha, simply add a splash of liquid chlorophyll (plain or mint-flavored) to make your water look more exceptional.

notes:

Ferments

Coconut Yogurt / contains coconut milk and probiotics; dairy-free and sugar-free

The elimination diet protocol is a great way to identify the foods that are responsible for your digestive symptoms, but it can be sad to say goodbye to your former favorite foods. If yogurt is one of the foods you miss, this coconut yogurt recipe will help you satisfy this craving without having to rely on dairy. This coconut milk recipe is delicious even without added sugar because of the natural sweetness of coconut—and you'll get a big dose of gut-friendly bacteria as a bonus.

Yields as much coconut yogurt as the amount of coconut milk you use:			
Basic	1 can (14 oz) ½-1 tsp	Coconut milk (additive-free) Probiotics (from a capsule or powder)	420 ml 2-5 ml
Optional	1 tsp ¼ cup + 2 Tbsp A few drops As desired	Gelatin Water Vanilla extract Fruits and/or nuts	5 ml 60 ml + 30 ml A few drops As desired

1. Pour your coconut milk into a Mason jar (1 pint or about 500 ml) or other similar glass bottle/container.
2. Add the probiotics of your choice. If your probiotics come in a capsule, just break it open to release the powder. Mix well by putting a lid on your glass container and shaking gently (or stir with a spoon).
3. Put your coconut milk in the oven, with the lid tightly closed. Make sure you won't need to use your oven for the next 24 hours. Leave your oven off, but turn the oven light on. This will generate the perfect temperature for your coconut milk to ferment.
4. Leave to ferment, undisturbed, for 24 hours.
5. After 24 hours, your coconut yogurt is ready. It's normal to observe a separation of the coconut milk into different layers. Simply mix your coconut yogurt (by shaking it with the lid on) and refrigerate it for at least 2-3 hours before consuming. The yogurt will be quite liquid and have the consistency of drinkable yogurt. If you want a thicker yogurt, follow the step 6. Otherwise, move to step 7.
6. Pour about 2 Tbsp (30 ml) of water (or coconut water) into a small bowl. Sprinkle the gelatin powder on top, forming a very thin layer. Meanwhile, heat ¼ cup (60 ml) of water or extra coconut milk in a small saucepan until hot (no need to boil it), and turn off the heat. Use a whisk or a fork to mix the gelatin into the cold water (it should have swollen and absorbed some water by that time). Pour the cold water and gelatin into the hot water, whisking constantly until well dissolved. Let sit for about 30 minutes until the gelatin mixture reaches room temperature. Add to your coconut yogurt to the Mason jar. Put the lid on and give it a gentle shake to mix evenly, and let sit in the fridge for 2-3 hours or until the gelatin sets.
7. Once cold, serve it with a few drops of vanilla, fresh or frozen fruits, nuts or unsweetened applesauce. Or use to serve with the Bananoatmeal (recipe, p. 28).

TIPS:

- **Avoid thickeners and BPAs.** Use coconut milk free of additives and thickeners like guar gum or carrageenan to prevent potential digestive issues. Coconut milk in a BPA-free can is also best. If you can't find good-quality coconut milk, make your own as explained on p. 226.
- **Coconut yogurt gummies!** If you want a thicker yogurt with an almost solid consistency (similar to gummies), use 1 Tbsp (15 ml) of gelatin. This can even be a fun project to do with the kids.
- **Coconut cottage cheese.** Follow all the same steps to make coconut yogurt, but use 1 Tbsp (15 ml) of gelatin powder in step 6. Let your coconut yogurt solidify for a few hours in the fridge, then use a fork or mixer to break the solidified yogurt into small pieces, giving it the appearance of cottage cheese. Sprinkle with a dash of salt and seasonings and serve as you would cottage cheese.

Fermented Pickles / contains cucumbers and probiotics

Traditionally prepared pickles used to be fermented for a few days to give them their tangy taste, but nowadays commercial pickles are simply marinated in vinegar. In addition to the sugar and other processed ingredients they contain, commercial pickles do not provide any of the beneficial bacteria found in traditionally fermented pickles, which can help balance your gut flora, boost your immune system, and assist your digestion. Making your own fermented pickles is easier than you think, and is a good way to incorporate more probiotics into your diet.

Yields about 2 cups (500 ml):		
8	Mini cucumbers (ideally organic and wax-free)	8
1.5-2 cups	Water (ideally filtered and chlorine-free)	325-500 ml
2 Tbsp	Unrefined salt	30 ml
A few sprigs	Fresh dill	A few sprigs
Optional	Other seasonings (peppercorn, garlic, hot chili, etc.)	Optional

1. Wash the mini cucumbers. Remove both ends and cut the cucumbers into halves or quarters. You can also leave them whole if you prefer (but you still need to cut off the ends).
2. In a sterile glass container, dissolve the salt in water.
3. Put a few sprigs of fresh dill and other seasonings at the bottom of a sterile Mason jar.
4. Add the mini cucumbers, packing them tightly. Cover with a few more sprigs of fresh dill.
5. Cover the mini cucumbers with the salt water. The content of the jar shouldn't be exposed to air to ensure a safe fermentation.
6. Put the lid on top without tightening it to allow gas formed by the fermentation to escape.
7. Repeat steps 3-6 if you have more mini cucumbers.
8. Let sit at room temperature for anywhere between 3 and 14 days. You will know that the fermentation has started once you see small bubbles (caused by the fermentation) rising at the top of the jar. You might need to open the jar and push the mini-cucumbers down if they rise above the water.
9. Once you feel like your fermented pickles are ready (taste to make sure they're just right for you), store in the fridge. This will stop the fermentation process. Your fermented pickles will keep for at least 3-6 months in the fridge.

TIPS:

- It's normal for a thin layer of white foam to appear at the top of the jar. Don't worry—simply remove it.
- If your fermented pickles don't smell good, throw them away because this might indicate the presence of harmful bacteria.
- Taste your pickles every few days to determine the right fermentation time for your taste.
- **Miss the vinegary taste?** Add a little of your favorite vinegar to your pickles once they've fermented.

Low-Sugar Kombucha

/ contains tea, probiotics (bacteria and yeast) and traces of sugar

Fermented foods are a powerful tool to balance your gut flora. Making your own ferments can also help you save a lot of money. Sauerkraut, fermented carrots and pickles, and yogurt (made with cow milk, goat milk, or coconut milk) are great examples of traditional fermented foods used in various cultures around the world to keep tummies happy. Kombucha is another tasty way to add more gut-friendly probiotics to your gut flora. Kombucha is a fermented tea that originated in northeast China over 2,000 years ago, and is made from a culture of up to 40 different strains of bacteria and yeast called a symbiotic culture of bacteria and yeast, or SCOBY. When making kombucha, your SCOBY will feed on the sugar, caffeine and other nutrients found in your tea to produce a deliciously thirst-quenching and gut-balancing beverage that comes with a nutritional bonus of B vitamins and antioxidants. The instructions may look pretty daunting, but don't worry—making kombucha is a lot simpler than it looks, especially after you've done it once or twice. In addition to making considerable savings, making your own kombucha also allows you to have more control on its sugar content.

Yields 1 gallon (16 cups or 4 L):			
Kombucha	1 1 gallon (16 cups) 4-8 2/3 cup ½ cup	Thick, healthy SCOBY (see p. 222) Water (ideally filtered and chlorine-free) Black or green tea bags (ideally organic) Sugar (ideally organic cane) Kombucha (from a previous batch)	1 4 L 4-8 180 ml 125 ml
Equipment	Big glass jars with a wide mouth and a plastic funnel for bottling Cheesecloth, towel or paper towel and rubber bands Wooden or plastic spoon (reserved for your kombucha to prevent contaminating it) Labels and pen		

Primary fermentation	Prepare the tea	1. Boil water in a kettle. Pour 4 cups into a large wide-mouth glass jar (with a capacity of at least 4 cups or 1 L) and add your tea bags. You can also use loose leaves if you prefer. Let steep for 20-30 minutes. 2. Remove the tea bags and add the sugar to the warm tea. Use your wooden spoon to stir your sweetened tea and make sure the sugar is completely dissolved. 3. Let your tea cool down to room temperature before adding the SCOBY. If you don't, you could kill your SCOBY!
	Add the SCOBY	4. Once your tea has reached room temperature, add the SCOBY sitting in ½ cup (125 ml) of your previous batch of kombucha. Don't worry if it sinks; you should see it floating again, or a new layer will form on top, within a few days. 5. Put some cheesecloth or a paper towel on top of your jar and secure it with a rubber band (your SCOBY needs to breathe!). Label your glass jar with the date on it so you remember when that batch was started.
	Let sit	6. Let the batch sit at room temperature, undisturbed, for 10-20 days. The fermentation time may vary depending on the temperature of your home and the size of your SCOBY. Taste it every day from day 10 to see if it has reached the desired taste (it will be ready once it doesn't taste sweet anymore).
	Bottle your kombucha	7. Once ready, use your kombucha wooden spoon or your cleaned hands and lift the SCOBY out of the jar. Place it in a small bowl with about ½ cup (125 ml) of kombucha. Your SCOBY is like a fish—it can't survive out of its tea! 8. Pour your kombucha into smaller glass bottles or Mason jars (2-4 cups or 0.5-1L), using your plastic funnel if needed (no metal for your SCOBY!). 9. Your kombucha is ready to drink. Simply keep it in the fridge and enjoy. If you don't want plain kombucha, follow the **secondary fermentation steps** below to add more fizz and flavors (optional).
	New batch!	10. Start a new batch of primary fermentation kombucha with your SCOBY.
Secondary fermentation	Flavor	11. Add about 1-4 Tbsp (15-60 ml) of fruit juice, fresh or frozen berries, puréed fruits per cup (250 ml) of kombucha. For example, you could try adding freshly grated ginger, lemon juice or whole fresh or frozen raspberries.
	Let sit	12. Tighten the caps on your kombucha bottles. The first fermentation is aerobic (requires oxygen) but the second fermentation is anaerobic (without oxygen). Let your flavored kombucha sit at room temperature for an extra 3-5 days, or until it's fizzy and tasty to your liking.
	Store	13. Once ready, keep your kombucha bottles in the fridge. 14. Enjoy a daily glass of kombucha (or more!).

Commercial kombucha usually contains at least 4-8 g of sugar (or about one to two teaspoons of sugar) per cup. You can decrease that amount by half by fermenting your kombucha over 2 weeks (14 days or more) and avoiding sugary fruits and fruit juice to flavor it during the secondary fermentation. Use ginger, lemon juice, mint, vanilla extract, hibiscus, cinnamon, lavender or chamomile to add flavor without any extra sugar! Raspberries are the best fruit option if you want to keep the sugar minimal.

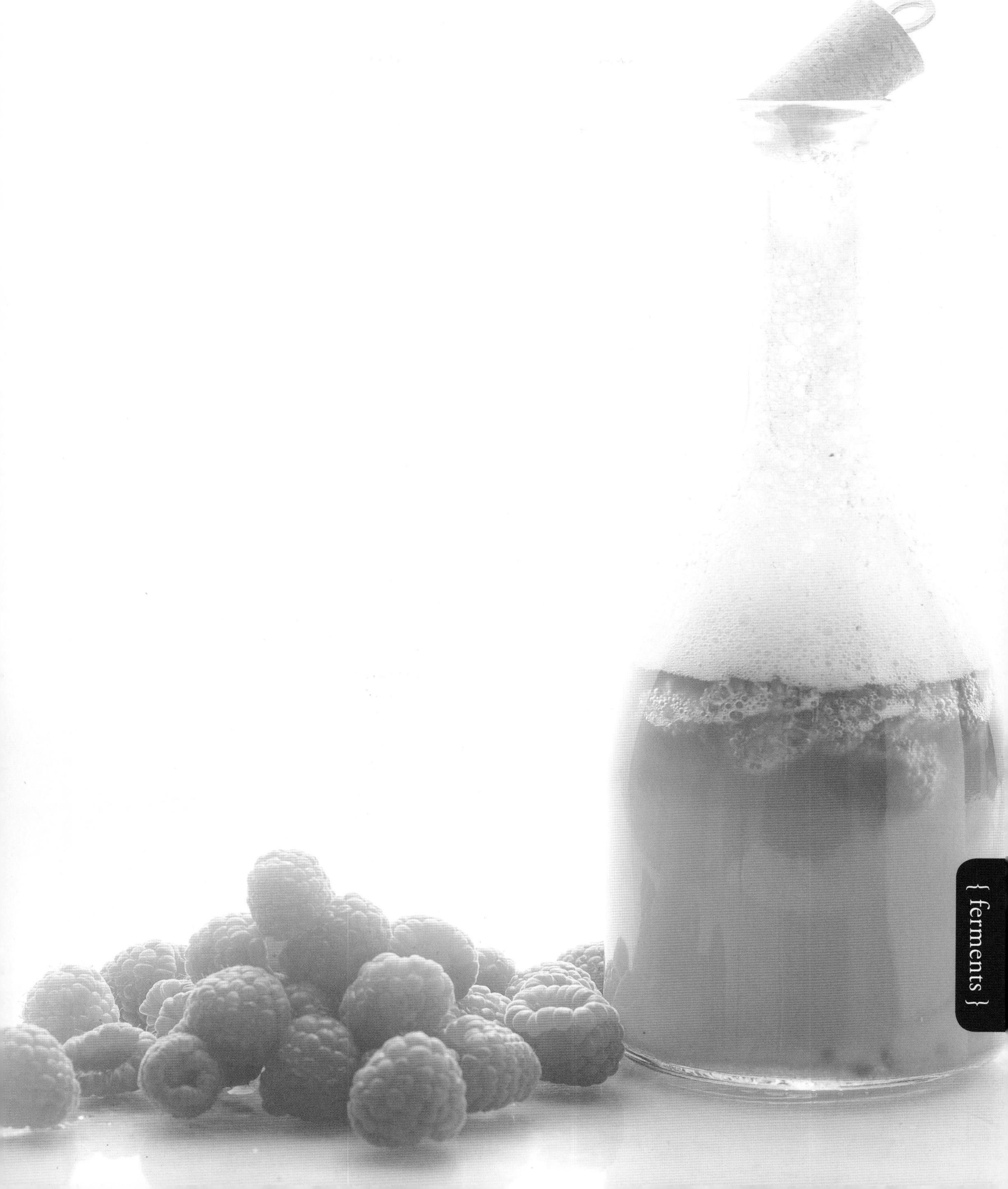

Special Projects

Project: Grow Your Own SCOBY

/ contains tea, probiotics (bacteria and yeast) and trace sugar

If you can't find a SCOBY to ferment your own Kombucha (recipe. p. 218), grow your own. It's a simple and fun project to do with the kids! All you need is a bottle of store-bought kombucha and a little patience... and you should be ready to make your first batch of probiotic-rich kombucha within a month.

Yields 1-2 baby SCOBYs:		
Kombucha culture	1 bottle	Store-bought kombucha, raw and plain (or the equivalent of homemade kombucha given from a friend)
Equipment		Bowl or small glass jar Cheesecloth, towel or paper towel, and rubber bands

1. Place 1-2 cups (250-500 ml) of kombucha in a small bowl or glass jar. You can start growing 2 baby SCOBYs with your bottle of store-bought kombucha if you separate the contents of your bottle into two small bowls. Label your bowls or jars with today's date.

2. Cover with a cloth, securing it with a rubber band, and let it sit at room temperature, undisturbed, for 1-3 weeks depending on the temperature of your home. You will first see a haze form, then a thin whitish film and finally a firmer jelly disk. Your baby SCOBY will be ready to brew its first batch of kombucha once it's about ¼ inch (0.5 cm) thick.

3. Train your baby SCOBY by starting with only a quarter of a batch of kombucha (using only 4 cups or 1 L of sweetened tea) while your SCOBY continues to grow and becomes ready for a full batch. If you try to make too big of a batch too soon, your SCOBY won't be able to control the pH of your kombucha and the sugar might attract undesirable microbes. To prevent mold formation, you can add 1-2 Tbsp (15-30 ml) of distilled white vinegar (optional). As your SCOBY grows bigger and stronger, start making half a batch of kombucha (using 8 cups or 2 L of sweetened tea) before making a full batch (using 16 cups or 4 L of sweetened tea).

TIPS:

- **Alternative to growing your own SCOBY?** Ask around! It's very likely that someone in your community already makes kombucha and could give you a baby SCOBY. You can also order one online.
- **SCOBY babies?** SCOBYs can also be called mushrooms or mothers. Every new batch of kombucha gives you SCOBY babies (the new layers forming on top of your SCOBY). You can use the new SCOBYs to increase your kombucha-making abilities by making more batches, or share them with friends. If you become overburdened with SCOBYs, simply compost them (or feed them to your pet).
- **Sampling your kombucha.** Use a straw and slide it down the side of your SCOBY, as deep as you can. Put your thumb on the top hole of your straw and take out your straw, holding your thumb in place. Put your straw over a small glass and release the liquid stuck in the straw by removing your thumb on top of it. Taste and decide whether it's ready or whether it requires a little bit more fermentation.
- **Caring for your SCOBY.** Remember that your SCOBY is alive! Avoid using anything metallic. Avoid direct sunlight (darkness or natural daylight are fine). Keep it away from smoke or house plants. Don't use herbal tea, as it won't work. Always cover your SCOBY with a cloth to protect it from insects or other contaminants while allowing it to breathe. If you see mold spots growing on your SCOBY, don't take any chances, and just discard it. Mold spots are usually blue or black and are located on top of the culture. Don't worry about white spots or films, strange texture, bubbles, or brown, slimy strings. If you see brown yeast strands forming under your SCOBY, simply remove them.
- **Store-bought kombucha** is sweeter because it's usually prepared with a lot of sugar and is fermented for only 10-12 days, which doesn't allow the SCOBY enough time to ferment all the sugar. Making your own kombucha gives you more control over the fermenting time to make sure you have minimal sugar left in your fermented tea before you drink it. Remember that the sugar you add to the tea is to feed the SCOBY, not you.
- **What's the best sugar to use?** There's no need to spend a fortune on the sugar you use to feed your SCOBY, as most of it will be fermented. That said, I still prefer using organic cane sugar to prevent my kombucha from being contaminated with traces of contaminants. I also prefer to stay on the safe side, considering that 95% of the white sugar produced in the USA comes from genetically modified (GMO) sugar beet crops. Less-processed sugar also contains traces of minerals that will enrich your kombucha.
- **Need a kombucha break?** Simply put your SCOBY in a bit of kombucha in the fridge (covered) to put it to sleep. Take it to room temperature when you're ready to make another batch.
- **Worried about caffeine?** Black and green tea do contain some caffeine, which can be a problematic ingredient if you suffer from digestive problems. The good news is that your SCOBY eats at least half of the caffeine found in the tea you use to make your kombucha, making it a relatively low-caffeine drink. For that reason, kombucha is usually fine to give to healthy children. If you're concerned about your caffeine intake, use green tea to prepare your kombucha since it naturally contains less than half of the caffeine of black tea. Fermenting your kombucha longer will also further reduce its caffeine content.
- **What about alcohol?** Although yeasts are known to produce alcohol during the fermentation process, a strain of bacteria found in the SCOBY ferments (eats) the alcohol produced by the yeasts, leaving very little alcohol in the final product. As a result, kombucha usually contains less than 0.5% alcohol, and is therefore classified as a non-alcoholic beverage. This is less than the 1-2% alcohol typically found in homemade kefir.
- **Storage.** Your ready-to-drink kombucha will keep in the fridge for 1-2 weeks, but don't wait too long because the fermentation process will continue and might turn your kombucha too vinegary. If it does turn to vinegar, you can use it for your salad dressings, as a hair rinse or facial toner, or even to clean your kitchen!

Homemade Coconut Butter / contains coconut

Although coconut butter is sometimes confused with coconut oil, they're not the same thing. Coconut oil refers only to the oil extracted from coconut and is 100 percent fat, while coconut butter is made of the whole white flesh of coconut that is ground into a paste. Coconut butter therefore contains some fats, as well as carbohydrates and fiber. Just like almond oil and almond butter. Coconut butter is sometimes also called coconut manna or coconut cream concentrate. Only coconut oil can be used for cooking, while coconut butter can be used more as a spread (and you'll find many uses for it in this cookbook). Coconut butter makes a tasty, convenient, concentrated source of energy. The only problem is that it doesn't come cheap. Making it yourself, even if you have to invest in a food processor or blender, could help you save a lot of money.

Yields about 1 ½ cup (375 ml):		
2 cups	Unsweetened dried coconut	500 ml
1-2 Tbsp	Coconut oil	15-30 ml

1. Put the unsweetened dried coconut flakes and 1 Tbsp (15 ml) of coconut oil in a food processor.
2. Blend for a few minutes, scraping down the sides once in awhile, until you get a paste. Depending on your blender, it may take up to 5-10 minutes. Check the consistency once in a while and give your blender a break if it starts to overheat.
3. Once you obtain a smooth and creamy consistency, add just enough coconut oil to get the right consistency.
4. Put in a glass jar and your homemade coconut butter should solidify at room temperature.

TIPS:

- If your homemade coconut butter becomes too hard, put the glass jar in a large bowl and fill it up with boiling water. Let rest 5-10 minutes and it should be easier to use.
- **Chocolate spread.** Mix a bit of coconut butter with unsweetened cocoa powder and honey or maple syrup, as tolerated, to get a delicious chocolate spread that you can eat by the spoon!
- **What to do with coconut butter?** Use your coconut butter in the Coconut Bark (recipe, p. 84), Coconut Fudge (recipe, p. 194), Coconut MCT Balls (recipe, p. 78), Energy Tea Latte (recipe, p. 208) and Baked Pear (recipe, p. 188) recipes. Or spread it on fruit slices or just enjoy it by the spoon.

notes:

Homemade Coconut Milk / contains coconut

It can be hard to find a high-quality coconut milk. Most coconut milks found in a carton are loaded with sugars and other processed ingredients. Some brands offer canned organic coconut milk, but the majority of them contain gut-irritating thickeners like guar gum, and only a handful of brands claim to be free of bisphenol A (BPA, a chemical in the plastic lining of most cans that can adversely affect your health). The only brand of coconut milk that is organic, BPA-free, and free of thickeners is Natural Value, but you have to order it online. Otherwise, just make your own coconut milk!

Yields about 1 cup (250 ml):		
1 cup	Unsweetened dried coconut (ideally organic)	250 ml
1 ½ cup	Hot water	375 ml

1. Place a metal colander with cheesecloth over a large bowl.
2. In a blender or food processor, blend the unsweetened dried coconut flakes and 1 cup (250 ml) hot water for about 2-3 minutes.
3. Strain the blended coconut in the cheesecloth.
4. Lift the cheesecloth and press the coconut pulp to extract all the liquid.
5. Return the pulp to the blender with an extra ½ cup (125 ml) of hot water.
6. Blend for another 1-2 minutes.
7. Strain the pulp in the same cheesecloth again and squeeze to extract all the liquid.
8. Get rid of the remaining pulp.
9. Keep your coconut milk for 4-5 days in the fridge.

TIPS:

- You can make a larger batch and freeze your coconut milk into individual servings to thaw as needed.
- **What to do with your coconut milk?** Use it in the Coconut-Asian Sauce (recipe, p. 168), Good-for-the-Tummy Tea (recipe, p. 206), Coconut Yogurt (recipe, p. 214), Breakfast Porridge (recipe, p. 38), Creamy Cream-Free Ice Cream (recipe, p. 184) and MCT Bomb Smoothie (recipe, p. 80).
- **There's always another way!** You can also make coconut milk simply by mixing roughly equal amounts of coconut butter (recipe, p. 224) with water. Strain the liquid with cheesecloth to get rid of the fiber if you want.

Indoor Herb Garden / appropriate for the elimination phase

Growing your own herbs helps you not only save money, but also boosts the flavors and antioxidant content of your meals. Dried herbs are definitely good, but I would take fresh herbs anytime when available. Freshness does make a difference. Ready to start your own herb garden and have your own supply of fresh herbs to add to your cooking? Give it a try and see how easy it is to have fresh herbs on hand. And you don't even need a green thumb!

1. Plant small herb plants or seeds in clean pots filled with potting soil. You don't need anything fancy: you can reuse old plastic or glass containers.
2. Leave your herbs in a sunny window and water them regularly.
3. Turn the pot once in a while so the plants get even light on all sides.
4. Wait until your plants reach at least 6 inches (15 cm) before harvesting the leaves.
5. Once your plants no longer have leaves, start over!

Here's a list of versatile herbs for your kitchen:

✓ Oregano	✓ Chives	✓ Parsley	✓ Sage
✓ Basil	✓ Dill	✓ Thyme	✓ Lemongrass
✓ Rosemary	✓ Mint	✓ Tarragon	✓ Coriander

Preserve Your Herbs / appropriate for the elimination phase

Whether you grow your herbs on your porch or in your kitchen, you may end up with more than you can use. Here are a few ways to preserve your extra fresh herbs.

Homemade Pesto	Frozen Herb Cubes
1. In a food processor or blender, process 2 cups (500 ml) fresh herbs with ¼-½ cup (60-125 ml) of extra-virgin olive oil until smooth.	1. Put small pieces of your fresh herbs in an ice cube tray.
2. Start with a small amount of oil and add more as needed to get the consistency right.	2. Fill with extra-virgin olive oil (or coconut oil) and freeze.
3. Keep your pesto in the fridge for 5-6 days or freeze it into small servings or in an ice cube tray.	3. Once frozen, remove the cubes of oil and herbs and transfer to a hermetic container or sealable plastic bag.
	4. Add your frozen herb cubes to soups or stews. Or add them to a skillet to stir-fry your vegetables or cook your eggs.

Frozen Liver Supplements:
The REAL "Flintstones" Vitamins

/ appropriate for the elimination phase

Are you worried that your diet may not be supplying you with all of the nutrients, vitamins and minerals your body need? Are you thinking about starting taking a multivitamin supplement? There's absolutely no need to if you eat 1-2 weekly servings of liver. Liver is Mother Nature's perfect multivitamin and offers the perfect ratio of the nutrients you need in their most bio-available forms. This includes minerals like iron, zinc, copper and selenium; vitamins A, D, K$_2$, E, C and the Bs; and choline. If you've tried the Bison Multivitamin (recipe, p. 120) or Liver Pâté (beef version, p. 120 of this cookbook or the chicken version on p. 294 of *DHwRF*) but still can't bring yourself to eat liver, then try these frozen liver pills! Simply pop a few of these supplements each day and you'll get your weekly serving of liver without having to cook or even taste it.

Yields up to 1 month's worth of liver pills:		
1 lb	Liver, fresh and raw	450 g

1. On a clean cutting board, cut your liver into very small cubes (about the size of a supplement that you can easily swallow without choking).
2. Place your liver supplements on a lined baking sheet, leaving enough space between each one to prevent them from sticking together in a huge block.
3. Freeze your liver for about 2 hours or until frozen solid.
4. Once your liver supplements are frozen, transfer them into a container or sealable bag. They shouldn't stick to each other at this point, but you can still use a bit of parchment or waxed paper in between to prevent this from happening.
5. Repeat steps 2, 3 and 4 if you didn't have enough room to freeze all of your liver supplements at once.
6. Label your frozen liver supplements with today's date and freeze them for at least 2 weeks (14 days). This step is important to kill potential pathogens (bacteria or parasites) that might be present in your raw liver (since you'll be eating it raw).
7. Once your frozen liver supplements have been frozen for at least 14 days, start popping a few every day to obtain your weekly serving of liver without even having to eat it!

TIPS:

- Find good-quality liver, ideally from healthy, pastured animals. Get to know your farmer, and don't be afraid to ask questions about what the animal was fed and how it was raised. It's your right to know. Knowing where your meat comes from makes it a lot safer for you to eat it raw and to trust its nutritional value.
- If your liver is already frozen when you buy it, leave it in the fridge for 3-4 hours to soften it a little and make it easier to cut. Then follow all the steps and re-freeze it for an extra 2 weeks before you start taking your frozen liver supplements.
- Make sure you don't choke on your liver pills! Swallow them with a glass of water. If they're too big to swallow, simply cut them into smaller pieces, even if they're frozen.
- If you're unsure of where your liver comes from, cook it prior to making your supplements.
- It's recommended to eat one to two weekly servings of 4-6 oz (120-180 g) of liver, so this recipe will give you enough frozen liver supplements to last 2-4 weeks.

Activated Nuts / contains nuts

If you have problems digesting nuts, try soaking them. The soaking process breaks down some of the anti-nutrients naturally found in nuts, making them easier to digest. You should definitely try this if you tend to see undigested pieces of nuts in your stools after eating them. Soaked nuts can also be called "activated" nuts. Think of them as being "activated" to work better with your digestive system. Properly preparing your nuts could be the missing step to help you successfully introduce them back into your diet (unless you have a true nut allergy, of course!).

1. Put your nuts in a large container, and fill it with water and about 1 tsp (5 ml) of unrefined salt. Make sure your container is large enough to account for the swelling of the nuts as they soak.
2. Change water once if using a longer soaking time.
3. Leave your nuts soaking at room temperature for 8-12 hours (or overnight).

Nuts	Soaking time	Dehydration time
Almonds		
Pepitas (pumpkin seeds)		
Pecans	8-12 hours or overnight	Oven: 12-24 hours Dehydrator: 8-12 hours
Walnuts		
Macadamia nuts		

1. Drain your nuts and pat dry on a towel.
2. Put on a baking sheet in the oven at the lowest temperature (no more than 150°F or 65°C) or in a food dehydrator (set at the lowest temperature). Dehydrate, turning occasionally, until your nuts are dry and crispy (see required dehydration time range in the table above). Or simply put your dry soaked nuts in your dehydrator overnight until crispy.

TIPS:

- **Blanching almonds.** You can also blanch almonds to remove their fibrous skin. Eat your blanched almonds as is or soak and dehydrate them to make their digestion even easier. All you need to do is put your almonds in a large bowl. Cover with boiling water. Let sit for no more than one minute. Drain and rinse under cold water. Pat dry with a towel and you should be able to easily slip off the skins between your fingers.
- **Caution:** if you're allergic to nuts, don't expect the activation process to help you tolerate them again. Whether nuts are raw, roasted or soaked, they retain the protein that can cause an allergic reaction.

Index

Activated charcoal	134
Activated nuts	232
Algae	124, 140
Alcohol	14, 210, 222
Alcohol-free drink	210
Almond flour	196
Almonds	15, 28, 50, 60, 168, 184, 196, 200, 224, 232
Animal protein	13, 18
Anti-inflammatory	13, 15
Apple	20, 78, 186, 188, 214
Apple cider vinegar	21, 98, 134, 154
Adrenal	14
Appetizers	53-91
Argentinean	154
Asafoetida powder	21, 116, 118, 146
Asian	104, 140, 168
Autoimmune	12, 112
Avocado	13, 14, 19, 20, 22, 42, 44, 46, 80, 82, 88, 98, 104, 110, 114, 118, 124, 126, 128, 130, 136, 138, 142, 144, 166, 170, 178, 184, 186
Bacon	36, 42, 44, 66, 72, 98, 102, 104, 106, 112, 120, 136, 144, 146, 200
Balsamic	21, 72, 102, 106, 108, 120, 146
Banana	28, 32, 48, 50, 80, 88, 90, 186, 190
Bark	84, 200
Barley	13, 14
Beans	13,18
Beef	13, 18, 22, 32, 68, 72, 101-115, 134, 136, 138,140, 144, 174
Beef heart	19, 108
Beef tongue	19, 114
Beer	14
Beets	62, 110, 112, 136, 144, 148
Benedict	44
Berries	14, 20, 28, 38, 72, 80, 82, 84, 86, 182, 184, 186, 190, 200, 202, 210, 218
Bison	13, 22, 104, 106, 110, 120, 230
Blended soup	54
Bone broth	54, 112, 118, 176
Bone marrow	19, 30, 62, 68
Bisphenol A (BPA)	130, 214, 226
Bread	13, 14, 36, 56, 106,114, 136, 138
Breakfast	18, 27-51
Breakfast cookies	50
Broth	54, 112, 118, 176
Burgers	106
Butter	13, 19, 22
Butternut squash	28, 40, 48, 54, 62, 80, 88, 106, 118, 144
BYO diet	16
Caffeine	14, 80, 84, 208, 218, 222
Carbonated water	210
Caramelized	102, 106, 114, 120, 152, 156, 162
Carrageenan	19, 214
Carrot	30, 40, 50, 54, 62, 76, 80, 88, 104, 106, 110, 112, 118, 124, 130, 134, 138, 140, 144, 146, 176, 196
Casein	14, 164

Cauli-bread	36, 56, 106,114, 136, 138
Cauli-bun	36, 44, 106
Cauliflower	36, 38, 44, 54, 56, 58, 60, 102, 114, 124, 134, 136
Cauli-pop	58
Cauli-rice	124, 140
Ceviche	126
Chai	208
Chicken	13, 18, 93-99, 104, 106, 134, 136,138, 140, 142, 144, 168, 170, 176, 190
Chickpea	60
Chili	14, 15, 21, 70, 72, 108, 126, 138, 168, 216
Chips	32, 60, 62, 68, 70
Chlorophyll	80, 210
Chocolate	14, 15, 48, 50, 84, 88, 90, 184, 186, 190, 196, 198, 200, 224
Chocolate cups	200
Choline	19, 42, 230
Cilantro	21, 98, 126, 142,144, 154, 178
Chimichurri	96, 102, 104, 108, 136, 154
Cinnamon	21, 28, 38, 48, 50, 54, 76, 78, 80, 90,118, 160, 164, 182, 186, 190, 206, 208,
Conjugated linoleic acid (CLA)	18, 164
Cocktail	14, 210
Cocoa powder	15, 48, 78, 84, 88, 90, 168, 182, 184, 186, 194, 196, 198, 200, 224
Coconut	13, 19, 28, 38, 50, 64, 78, 80, 82, 84, 88, 90, 140, 168, 182, 184, 188, 190, 192, 194, 196, 198, 206, 208, 214, 224, 226
Coconut aminos	21, 70, 72, 102, 104, 124, 140, 160, 168
Coconut butter	28, 50, 78, 80, 84, 188, 194, 208, 224, 226
Coconut cream	198
Coconut cream concentrate	See coconut butter
Coconut flour	40, 50, 54, 88, 90, 196
Coconut ghee	160
Coconut manna	See coconut butter
Coconut milk	22, 38, 54, 80, 82, 86, 140, 168, 184, 186, 190, 192, 206, 214, 226
Coconut oil	13, 19, 22, 32, 84, 160, 208
Coconut sugar	50, 86, 198, 200, 206
Coconut water	80, 192, 198, 214
Coconut, dried shredded	28, 48, 50, 64, 78, 84, 90, 186, 194, 196, 198, 200
Coffee	14, 15, 208
Cookies	50, 182, 196
Cooking banana	See plantain
CoQ10 (coenzyme Q10)	108
Corn	13, 18, 19, 20, 58, 128
Cottage	214
Cravings	62, 70, 76, 86, 134,164, 182, 200, 202, 214
Crock-Pot	114, 118, 134, 160, 174, 176
Cumin	15, 21, 32, 60, 108
Curry	14, 15, 21
Dairy	13, 14, 17, 18, 46, 54
Dehydrator	62, 70, 72, 178, 232
Deli meat	98, 138
Dentist	134
Desserts	181-203
Digestive Health with REAL Food (DHwRF) book	10, 11, 15, 16
Digestive Health with REAL Food (DHwRF) protocol	16-18

Digestive symptoms	11-12, 16-17, 134
Dressing	98, 144, 166, 178
Dried fruit	14, 48, 50, 72, 78, 84, 88, 90, 194, 196, 200
Dried shredded coconut	28, 48, 50, 64, 78, 84, 90, 186, 194, 196, 198, 200
Duck fat	19, 22
Ecuadorian	32, 126, 142
Egg-free	28-33, 90
Eggplant	14, 20, 44, 62, 106, 112, 136, 148, 172
Egg whites	182
Egg yolks	19, 42, 98, 110, 114, 134, 138, 170, 198, 208
Eggs	13-15, 18, 22, 36, 38, 40, 42, 44, 46, 48, 50, 56, 60, 64, 66, 88, 98, 106, 136, 138, 142, 144, 168, 170, 172, 182, 196
Elimination diet	11, 15, 16, 17, 21, 72, 90
Elimination phase	16
Epsom salt bath	134
Fajitas	114
Ferments	213-220, 222
Fish	123-131
Flax seeds	15, 90
FODMAPs	11-18, 21
Food list	13-15, 20, 21, 22
Food quality	22
French	44, 110, 170, 172, 198, 200
Fritters	40
Frozen treats	82, 184, 186, 202
Fruit	13-16, 19-20, 22, 40, 48, 50, 78, 80, 82, 84, 86, 88, 90, 168, 184, 188, 190, 192, 194, 196, 198, 200, 210, 214, 218
Fruit, dried	See dried fruit
Fudge	194
Garden	228
Garlic	14, 21, 54, 60, 72, 96, 98, 102, 108, 116, 126, 142, 146, 154, 156, 162, 168, 176
Gelatin	18-19, 80, 86, 134, 208, 214
Ghee	13, 19, 22, 76, 128, 158, 160, 162, 164
GI symptoms	11-12, 16-17, 134
Ginger	21, 50, 54, 66, 72, 104, 124, 140, 160, 164, 168, 206, 218
Gluten	11-15
Gluten-free	11-15
Grain-free	11-15
Grains	11-15
Grass-fed	13, 18, 19, 22, 102, 110, 118, 120, 134, 160, 174, 208
Grilled fruits	190
Ground meat	40, 72, 104, 106, 110, 112, 120, 136, 138, 146
Guacamole	36, 96, 102, 104, 106, 108, 114, 128, 130, 138, 166
Guar gum	19, 54, 184
Gummies	86, 214
Gums	See guar gum
Gut flora	14, 15, 216, 218
Gut-healing	15, 30, 80, 134, 208
Ham	36, 44
Heart	19, 108
Herb	13, 20, 21, 22, 128, 136, 154, 158, 178, 228
Hollandaise	44, 170
Homemade bone broth	54, 112, 118, 176, 192, 206, 214, 226
Honey	40, 48, 50, 76, 78, 80, 82, 84, 86, 116, 182, 184, 186, 188, 190, 192, 194, 196, 206, 224

Hummus	60
IBS	12
Ice cream	14, 184, 186
Imitation crab	124
Ingredients	13-15, 18-22
Iodine	70, 140
Italian	112, 136, 144, 146, 148
Japanese	124
Jerky	72
Jicama	40, 106, 110
Kebabs	60, 98, 190
Kelp	21, 140
Kombucha	210, 218, 222
Lactose	14
Lamb	104, 106, 118, 120
Lard	13, 19, 22, 174
Lasagna	148
Latte	14, 206, 208
Leaky gut	12, 14, 15
Legumes	13, 14, 16
Lemon	21, 42, 60, 84, 96, 110,116, 126, 128, 130, 144, 164, 166, 170, 194, 210, 218
Lengua	114
Lentils	13
L-glutamine	80, 134, 208
Liquid diet	134
Liver	19, 56, 62, 120, 230
Low-FODMAP	11
Marrow	See bone marrow
Master list	23-25
Mayonnaise	21, 138, 142, 166, 178
Medium-chain triglycerides (MCT)	78, 80, 206
Meatballs	104, 146
Meringue	182
Mexican	114, 166
Monosodium glutamate (MSG)	72, 116, 140, 176
Muffins	66, 88, 90
Multivitamins	120, 230
Mushroom	20, 44, 64, 66, 104, 106, 112, 136, 138, 140, 146, 148, 222
Mustard	15, 21, 110, 116
Nightshades	13, 14, 15, 21, 46, 70, 72, 112, 146, 172
Nightshade-free	72, 112, 148
Noodle bowls	140
Nori	21, 70, 124, 138
Nuts	15, 19, 22, 28, 38, 48, 50, 84, 88, 140, 168, 196, 200, 232
Nutrient-dense	15, 16, 18-22
Oatmeal	13, 28, 38
Offal	19, 30, 68, 108, 114, 120, 176
Oils	13, 19, 22
Olive oil	13, 199
Olives	104, 106, 136
Omega-3 fats	18, 128, 130
Omega-6 fats	13, 18, 19
Onions	16, 20, 21, 106, 110, 114, 120, 126, 152, 172,176

Organic	19, 20, 22, 216, 218, 222, 226
Organ meat	19, 30, 68, 108, 114, 120, 176
Paleo	11, 12
Pancakes	48
Paprika	14, 21, 70, 72, 112
Parsnip	40
Pasta	13, 112, 140, 144, 146, 148
Pasteurized	15
Pastured	13, 18, 19, 22
Pâté	19, 56, 62, 120, 230
Peanuts	13
Pear	188, 190
Peppers	14, 15, 20, 21
Peruvian	118, 126, 142
Pesto	136, 228
Pickles	216
Pizza	136
Plantain	32, 48, 62, 88, 126
Popsicles	82
Pork	13, 22, 98, 138, 140, 116
Porridge	28, 38
Portobello mushroom	44, 106, 136
Potage	54
Potato	14, 20
Probiotics	82, 214, 216, 218, 222
Problematic foods	13-15
Processed foods	13-15
Produce	19-20
Prosciutto	36, 42, 44, 98, 104, 136, 138
Protein	13-15, 18-19
Protocol	16-17
Pumpkin	28, 80, 232
Quality	22
Ranch dressing	98
Ratatouille	46, 172
REAL food	18-22
Recipe list	6-8, 23-25
Recovery	134
Reintroduction phase	16-17, 18, 21
Ribs	116
Rice	13, 38, 56, 124, 140
Rooibos tea	208
Rye	13, 14
Salad dressing	98, 144, 166, 178
Salads	98, 130
Salmon	124, 128, 130
Salsa	114, 138, 190
Salt	13, 16, 18, 20, 21, 22
Sandwich	36, 138
Sauces	98, 151-179
SCOBY	222
Seasonings	20-21
Seaweed	70, 124, 140
Seeds	15, 21, 22, 50, 60, 90, 168, 228, 232

Sesame seeds	15, 60
Shrimp	124, 136, 140, 142, 144, 168,
Side dishes	32, 40, 54, 56, 58, 60, 62, 70, 172
Slow cooker	114, 118, 134, 160, 174, 176
Slush	202
Smoked salmon	124, 136
Smoothie	80
Snacks	28-91, 176, 182, 186, 190, 196, 202, 206, 208, 214, 216, 218
Soaking	232
Soups	54, 134
Soy	13, 15, 18, 19
Spaghetti	16-17, 30, 112, 144, 146
Spices	20-21
Spinach	20, 30, 36, 44, 64, 66, 106, 130, 136
Spiralized vegetables	112, 118, 140, 144, 146
Steak	102, 110
Steak tartare	110
Stew	118, 134, 172
Stir-fry	140
Sugar	14
Sunflower seeds	15, 50, 168
Supplements	120, 230
Surgery	134
Surimi	124
Sushi	124
Sweet potato	14, 16, 20, 30, 40, 44, 50, 62, 104, 106, 110, 118, 120, 126, 144, 148
Tahini	60
Tallow	13, 19, 22, 40, 174
Tamari sauce	21, 70, 124, 140, 168
Tartare	110
Tea	206, 208
Tempura	124
Thickeners	19, 22, 82, 184, 192, 206, 214, 226
Tomato	14, 15, 20, 21, 36, 44, 46, 54, 66, 104, 106, 112, 114, 136, 138, 146, 148, 172
Tongue	114
Treats	181-203
Turmeric	54, 58, 80, 206, 208
Variety	13, 18, 22
Vegetable chips	62
Vegetables	14, 19-20, 22
Vinegar	13, 21
Wasabi	124
Watermelon	14, 20, 202
Weston A. Price Foundation (WAPF)	18
Whipped cream	192
Wild-caught fish	13, 22, 128
Wine	14, 146
Wrap	138
Yogurt	214
Zucchini	20, 40, 44, 50, 62, 112, 118, 144, 146, 148, 172, 196
Zucchini noodles	112, 140, 144, 146

Digestive Health with REAL Food, by Aglaée Jacob, MS, RD, provides a roadmap to help you address the root causes of your digestive issues. It also contains 60+ recipes, each with a mouth-watering full color photo, charts, food lists and meal plans.